THE ARABIC PLAYS OF
KAHLIL GIBRAN

Translation by Abdullah Halawani
and Abdelmalek Halawani
Arabic Editor: Manal Barakat, M.A.
Nicholas Martin, Editor

D1566175

First printed edition, September 2015

ISBN-13: 978-0692465455
ISBN-10: 0692465456

Printed in the United States of America

First Kindle edition, September 2015

Cover designs by True Turner Tidwell,
from original artwork by Kahlil Gibran.

THE ARABIC PLAYS OF KAHLIL GIBRAN

CONTENTS

ILLUSTRATIONS

INTRODUCTION

Kahlil Gibran is surely one of the most well-known and widely read authors of all time. Born in Bsharri, Lebanon, in 1883, he emigrated to the United States in 1895 and spent most of his life in Boston and then New York, where he died in 1931 at the age of only 48. He is best known for his book, *The Prophet,* which "is one of the most beloved spiritual classics of our time. It has sold millions of copies in more than forty languages since it was first published in 1923."[1] Few would doubt that it will forever stand as his greatest achievement and one that eclipses his great many other works.

Most who know Gibran are aware that he wrote other books, poems, and articles and that he was also a respected artist whose illustrations accompany nearly all of his printed works. But very few know that he ever wrote plays, which is perhaps not surprising given that none ever appeared in English until well after his death.

Most of Gibran's literary works were originally written in Arabic, although *The Prophet* was written in English, as were most of his later works, beginning with *The Madman* in 1918. Only a few of Gibran's Arabic works were ever translated into English prior to the late 1940s, when Lebanese-born

---

[1] Knopf Doubleday website, http://knopfdoubleday.com/book/59590/the-prophet (15 June 2015).

Anthony Rizcallah Ferris of Austin, Texas, began translating large quantities of his works, which he continued to do until his own death in 1962. Among the extensive Gibran materials that Ferris helped bring to the English-speaking world for the first time were two plays. One was *Iram, the City of Lofty Pillars,* which appeared in the 1947 collection, *The Secrets of the Heart,* published by The Philosophical Library in New York.[2] The other was *Assilban,* which first appeared in the 1962 *Spiritual Sayings of Kahlil Gibran,* another publication of The Philosophical Library. The play was named for the lead character, Paul Assilban, no doubt an Anglicizing of the Arabic Bulus al-Sulban.

A few references to Gibran's plays appear in the remarkable biography, *Kahlil Gibran, His Life and World,* first published by the New York Graphic Society in 1974. The book was written by Gibran's cousins, who also saw into print for the first time the only plays that Gibran completed in English. The first was *Lazarus and His Beloved,* published in 1973 by the New York Graphic Society and, in London, by William Heinemann. The second was *The Blind,* which was included when *Lazarus* was republished in 1981 in a volume entitled *Dramas of Life: Lazarus and His Beloved and The Blind,* published by the Westminster Press of Philadelphia.

---

[2] The play does not appear in all editions of *Secrets of the Heart;* the 1971 Philosophical Library edition, for example, is only a "special selection." *Iram* does, however, appear in a reprint of the 1947 edition by The Citadel Press (New York, 1992), which had also included it in its 1951 *A Treasury of Kahlil Gibran.* Another and more recent translation appears in *Visions of the Prophet,* Frog Ltd., a division of North Atlantic Books, Berkeley, California. There it appears as *The Many-columned City of Iram* and is a 1995 translation from French by Margaret Crosland, based on Jean-Pierre Dahdah's translation from Arabic in: Kahlil Gibran, *Visions du Prophète* (Monaco: Editions du Rocher, 1995).

According to the cousins, the manuscripts of the two English plays were among boxes of materials bequeathed by Gibran to his close friend and sponsor, Mary Haskell. She in turn gave them to Gibran's sister, Marianna, who never married but "regarded as her own the children of her cousins Nicholas and Rose."[3] The five children of Nicholas and Rose were apparently all named by Gibran, and the middle son was his namesake, often referred to as "Kahlil, the sculptor" to minimize the inevitable confusion with Kahlil, the poet. It was Kahlil, the sculptor, and his wife, Jean, who not only made possible the publishing of Gibran's English plays, but also painstakingly developed their landmark biography, without which very little would be known about the poet (and playwright), Kahlil Gibran.

Lazarus and His Beloved presents a conversation between the resurrected Lazarus of the New Testament and his mother and sisters.[4] The unexpected twist is that Lazarus is not at all pleased to have been brought back to life. Instead, he is most despondent, having been in paradise with his beloved and now forced to separate from her and return to the emptiness of life on earth. Copyright restrictions prevent the play from being included in this volume, but it is readily available from bookstores and libraries, and it has been posted on the Internet in its entirety by several sources.

In their introduction to the 1973 edition, reprinted in the 1981 edition, Jean and Kahlil, the sculptor, Gibran provide historical perspectives on both Gibran's life and the play itself, revealing that Gibran first wrote his story of Lazarus as a prose poem in

---

[3] Kahlil Gibran, *Dramas of Life: Lazarus and His Beloved and The Blind* (Philadelphia: Westminster Press, 1981), 31-33.

[4] Jesus raises Lazarus from the dead in the Gospel of John, chapter 11.

Arabic about 1914. He had developed it into a play in English by 1926, when he shared it with Mary Haskell.[5] Although he read it to a live audience in 1929, it did not (as mentioned) appear in print until published by the cousins in 1973.[6]

The second English play, *The Blind,* centers around the real meaning of blindness by contrasting the exceptionally perceptive David Rugby, who has lost his physical sight, with his wife, Helen, who sees perfectly well on a physical level but is spiritually and emotionally blind. As are all of Gibran's plays, the work is short and in only one act. It was probably written in 1926; the cousins reveal that he discussed it "in embryo form" with Mary Haskell in May of that year.[7] Copyrights prevent its inclusion in this volume, but it is readily available through bookstores and libraries. It has also been posted on the Internet.[8]

In their introduction to *Dramas of Life,* the cousins wrote that among Gibran's effects were also three unfinished manuscripts entitled *The Banshee, The Last Unction,* and *The Hunchback or The Man Unseen,* "with no contemporaneous clues as to their dates."[9] These are now housed at the Soumaya

---

[5] Kahlil Gibran, *Lazarus and His Beloved—A One-Act Play* (London: William Heinemann, 1973), 19. Lazarus as a prose poem appears on pages 117-121 of *The Eye of the Prophet,* a collection of Gibran's writings published by Frog, Ltd., Berkeley, California, in 1997. The poem was translated from French by Margaret Crosland. It had been translated into French from Arabic by Jean-Pierre Dahdah in: Kahlil Gibran, *L'Oeil du Prophete* (Paris: Albin Michel, 1991).

[6] A passage from the original manuscript, in Gibran's own handwriting, is reproduced in both editions but more fully in the 1981 volume of *Dramas of Life, op. cit.,* 24-25.

[7] *Op. cit.,* 36.

[8] Museo Soumaya website, http://gibrankgibran.org/eng/textos-ineditos/el-ciego (7 June 2015).

Museum in Mexico City and have been posted in their entirety at the Museum website.[10]

The Banshee is more of a plot summary than a play *per se*. It has no dialogue, and it seems that Gibran simply recorded in some detail what he envisioned but never completed. The basic story line is that the hero, Padraic O'Shaugnessey, is a poet at heart, and yet circumstances and those around him have hindered him from expressing his real, inner nature. He feels himself a prisoner with a continual longing to be free. He converses with the Dark Woman from the forest, who calls him to his true expression as he follows her into death.

The Last Unction is a more finished play, requiring little more than final editing. It is very similar to Gibran's Arabic prose poem, "Behind the Curtain," which was published in 1916. The poem was translated by Anthony Ferris and appears in the aforementioned *Secrets of the Heart,* and the play is an almost identical story. In it, a priest administers the last unction to a dying woman. After she dies and while her sorrowful husband sleeps in an adjoining room, the priest confesses his lifelong love for the woman and prays for forgiveness.

The Man Unseen is one of the few works that Gibran wrote in both Arabic and English, and probably about the same time. Although never published in its English version, it *was* published in Arabic, and it is translated here as it appeared in 1927. It differs very little from the English version, which has been posted on the Internet by the Soumaya Museum.[11]

---

[9] Kahlil Gibran, *Dramas of Life, op. cit.,* page 36.
[10] Museo Soumaya website, http://gibrankgibran.org/eng/textos-ineditos (7 June 2015).
[11] Museo Soumaya indicates that this play had formerly been entitled

The present work came about as a series of "happy accidents" that now, in retrospect, seem quite remarkable. Having read *Dramas of Life* and learned of the existence of the unfinished manuscripts, I began an Internet search for information about them. At that time (2013), the Soumaya Museum had not yet posted them, and it was virtually impossible to find out anything more. Among the very few Internet hits, though, was a rather obscure footnote in a Spanish-language biography that made reference to *Dramas of Life* and also mentioned the unfinished plays by name.[12] The footnote also revealed that there were five unpublished Arabic plays that had appeared in a collection released by Dar Amwaj of Beirut in 1993.[13] As a long-term student of Gibran, I just had to know what was in that Arabic book. I had no idea there were still works of his that had never been translated into English, and I was bound and determined to find out what they were and what they said.

I was able to order a copy from a book dealer in Beirut with an English-language website. I then

---

The Hunchback and that a page is missing. The Arabic version, which is translated here, is complete.

[12] The footnote appeared in a Spanish translation of Robin Waterfield's *Prophet, The Life and Times of Kahlil Gibran* (London: The Penguin Press, 1998), 340, footnote 83 (in the Spanish, page 371, footnote 80).

[13] That collection is المجموعة خارج نصوص جبران، خليل جبران *Gibran Khalil Gibran, Nosous Kharej al-Majmou'a,* (Texts Outside of the Collection), ed. Antoine al-Qawwal (Beirut: Dar Amwaj, 1993). By "Outside of the Collection" is meant those writings not included in the classic *The Complete Collection of Works of Gibran Khalil Gibran* (in Arabic), compiled by Mikhail Naima (in English, Naimy); one of several editions was published by Sader of Beirut in 2011. Note the Arabic rendering of Gibran's full name, in contrast to the English and more familiar "Kahlil Gibran," which reverses the *a* and *h* and drops the first "Gibran."

began a search for Arabic translators who could help me make sense of it, because I didn't speak a word. The search proved far more difficult than I would ever have imagined, but in response to an advertisement I had posted in the Dallas, Texas, Craigslist, Abdullah Halawani of Jerusalem sent an email and offered his services. A very effective working partnership was formed, a grand adventure began, and the current volume gradually came into being. His brother, Abdelmalek, served as co-translator, and the finished work was later reviewed and fine-tuned with the help of Manal A. Barakat of Amman, Jordan. Manal received her Master's degree in Arabic-English translation from Durham University in England and provides freelance translation services to members of the international banking, corporate, and diplomatic communities.

All of us working together on this book have felt deeply honored to have the opportunity to make a contribution to the legacy of Kahlil Gibran. With thankfulness and great joy, we now share it with you.

NRMM
Plano, Texas
June 15, 2015

THE PLAYS OF KAHLIL GIBRAN
with probable dates of writing

IN ARABIC

The Beginning of the Revolution (1914)
The Colored Faces (1916)
Between Night and Morning (1918)
Al-Sulban (1920)
Iram of the Pillars (1923)
The Man Unseen (1927)
The King and the Shepherd (1930)

IN ENGLISH

Lazarus and His Beloved (1926)
The Blind (1926)
The Man Unseen (1927)
The Banshee (unknown)
The Last Unction (unknown)

THE ARABIC PLAYS OF KAHLIL GIBRAN

EDITOR'S NOTE: Every effort has been made to present Gibran's Arabic plays as literally as reasonably possible while preserving a grammatically correct English. No capitalization and little punctuation appear in the Arabic, and variation is always possible in the transliteration of Arabic words, names, and places. Some liberties have been taken with the layout, italics, and parentheses for purposes of clarity and consistency. All footnotes and bracketed insertions are my own unless otherwise noted. A few editorial comments appear in the Arabic source material; these are presented here as footnotes but always indicate when they were made by the Arabic editors, Antoine al-Qawwal or Mikhail Naima.

1

THE BEGINNING OF THE REVOLUTION [1914] [14]

THE SCENE: A café by the sea, Beirut
THE TIME: A rainy day in February 1914
THE CAST: Ahmed Beik, a Muslim
                Farid Effendi, a Christian[15]

The curtains open on Farid Effendi, a Christian, and Ahmed Beik, a Muslim, seated at a table with some food and drinks.

Farid Effendi: How clever these Turks are, and how deep their knowledge of Syrian wit and Arab values! They know where in the Syrian body the illness lies. Then they pour their concoctions of deception on it and sprinkle their cunning powders over it.

---

[14] Al-Qawwal notes that this play was published by John Dayeh in his [Arabic] book, *Aqidat Gibran* [The Doctrine of Gibran], pages 249-251, as taken from Gibran's documents in the library of [the University of] North Carolina.

    The play had appeared in the March 9, 1914 edition of *As-Sayeh* [The Tourist] (Robin Waterfield, *op. cit.,* page 323, footnote 54); the journal was active from 1912-31 (*op. cit.,* 97).

[15] *Effendi* is a general term of respect. "Farid Effendi" is as if saying, "honorable (or esteemed) Farid." At times only *Effendi* is used, as if addressing someone as *sir.*

Ahmed Beik: By God, don't call the Turk clever. Say, instead, that the Syrian is a blind and lost boy walking in pitch darkness. If he catches sight of a distant lantern, he mistakes it for the sun or the moon. No, the Turk is not clever, but it's the idiocy of the Arab Syrian that makes the foolishness of others seem like knowledge and brilliance.

Farid Effendi: Listen, my friend, for two years now, the cream of the Syrian intellect has been rising over a zealous flame of enthusiasm. It is spreading out on a platter of freedom and reform and the lofty principles that produced Jean-Jacques Rousseau, Voltaire, Patrick Henry, and Garibaldi, and others who have created monuments of freedom in the hearts of the people in the West. Today, the Turk stretches out his long arm and pours over this cream a mixture of that magical drug that has been developed by the minds of the Ottoman politicians since the beginning of the nineteenth century. This drug appears at one moment in the form of molasses and at another in the form of tar. If today the greatest chemist tried to extract that cream from between the Turkish tar and molasses, he would not be able to find a way to do it.

Ahmed Beik: What you say reminds me of an article I read by Kahlil Gibran about narcotics and scalpels,[16] and I don't consider you

---

[16] See *Narcotics and Dissecting Knives,* translation by Anthony Ferris, in *A Second Treasury of Kahlil Gibran* (New York: Citadel Press, 1962); also in *The Treasured Writings of Kahlil Gibran* (Edison, New Jersey:

anything but an exaggerator, just like that writer who views the Middle Eastern situation through dark glasses.

Farid Effendi: Yes, I'm aware of the views of that Syrian writer, and there was a time when I thought he was one of those people who tend to overstate issues and cannot see an end to the Eastern night or a spring for the Syrian winter. But now I see the logic in his opinions, and I even emulate him.

Ahmed Beik: Don't exaggerate. Instead, let's look at the present situation the way a doctor would look at a sick patient. You ascribe intelligence to the Turk and idiocy to the Syrian, whereas I would ascribe mulishness to both.

Farid Effendi: What do you mean by that?

Ahmed Beik: I am a Muslim, with Eastern, Muslim values, but I have lived for quite some time in Europe. During this time, I have seen the magnificence of Islam and its significance for modern civilization. When I came back, I felt like a stranger in my homeland, homeless among my family and friends. However, I did not turn a blind eye to the glory of Islam when I stood surrounded by the blind among Muslims. And I am not despairing about the future of the Middle East though standing amid the crippled of them.

The Middle East is a great reality, and Islam is a great reality too, while mulishness is part of the Turkish effort

Castle Books, 1985).

to put a bridle on Arab powers. And what is the relationship of the Arab powers to Islam except the relationship of the heart to the body?

This mulishness is evident when Arabs, a starving nation, settle for as little as chewing on radish leaves when the bread of life fills plains and valleys. The Turkish monopoly of power drives it towards total destruction and annihilation, while the gratification of the aristocratic Syrian, who is thought to be a reformer, with a position in the House of Lords, takes him unwittingly closer to a twenty square-foot donkeys' stable that is built by Ottoman politicians for all those who hold their heads up to the sky while their legs are sinking underwater. This is the philosophy of mulishness.

Farid Effendi: By God, I am truly impressed, Ahmed Beik! You are really well-versed in the nature of livestock!

Ahmed Beik: Yes, those people are no different than camels, donkeys, and mules. When I think of that eagle that once spread his wings from Andalusia to the heart of China, and see it today bound in chains forged by the hands of Arab and Turkish fools, my soul goes into a state of turmoil inside me and my head reels. In that moment, I wish that Khalid bin al-Walid could be resurrected from his grave to break these chains around the feet of the noblest eagle in history— those chains that are tied to the legs of Islam, which moved heaven and earth for science, created the glory of Damascus, Bagdad, Basra, Cairo, and Granada, transformed bin al-'As into a leader, made bin Khaldoon a philosopher, and raised al-Mutanabbi to be a poet.

Farid Effendi: I'm convinced by all you've said, Ahmed Beik. Islam is a magnificent reality. It should stay pure and free from all superfluous matters that rid it of its power and vitality.

Ahmed Beik: The nature of Islam does not accept superfluousness. Islam is an abstract and absolute truth. If Muslims turn away from Islam towards superfluous matters, then that is not the result of a moral ailment in Islam, as some Westerners believe. It is an ailment in Muslims. Keep in mind that Islam is not just a religion, as English orientalists[17] imagine, but it is a religion and also a civil law that encompasses beneath its tremendous wings all the needs of human beings in every era. A true Muslim, while following a spiritual fervor, is also an element of a civil community and a magnificent tradition.

Farid Effendi: Well said, Beik. And the Christian attributes to Christianity all that you have attributed to Islam. He considers it a spiritual religion but also sees it as the foundation of the European and American civilizations.

Ahmed Beik: Everyone has the freedom to think and say whatever he wishes. But I've found that truth supports the speech of one

---

[17] "Orientalists" in the sense of those who study the Middle East.

person and divorces itself from the speech of another.

Farid Effendi: What do you mean? Do you think that the truth discredits the statement of a European who says that Christianity created modern civilization?

Ahmed Beik (remains silent for a moment then says reluctantly): Do you think that the truth supports nations that speak highly of the teachings in their churches while at the same time directly contradicting those teachings in their political institutions, war departments, and every place where activities are initiated by the West? I respect Christianity as a religion, but I cannot equate Christianity with the actions of the Christians. That's the difference between Christianity and Islam. Islam teaches and acts in accordance with its teachings. But Christianity doesn't do that.

A Christian loves his enemy when he's at church, but when he leaves, he begins to think of effective ways to exterminate his enemies. A Christian glorifies poverty, humility, and peacefulness when sitting in front of his Bible, but the moment he sets his book aside, he puffs himself up, boasting of his wealth, flaunting his grandeur, and showing off his ignorance. A Christian bows his head and lifts up his arms and proclaims with a sound equal to the sighs of the Virgin Mary, "And whosoever shall smite thee on thy right cheek, turn to him the other also," but then he erupts like a hungry lion, declaring that "in every harbor in my country, there are armored vehicles carrying guns with triggers that harvest souls. He who dares to touch with insult the hem of my robe shall die a bitter death."

A Christian chants, "Let us be like the lilies of the field that neither toil nor spin yet live under the sun with a glory never seen by Solomon." Yet we see the Christian devising subtle tricks that draw silver and gold from the pocket of his next of kin and into his own.

A Christian says that life is nothing and afterlife is everything but lives for the present and doesn't think of the afterlife.

Yes, by God, I respect Christianity, and yet I agree with the words of Nietzsche, "There was only one Christian, and he died on the cross." And I repeat the words of Kahlil Gibran, "If Jesus of Nazareth returned to this world, he would die hungry, estranged, and alone." This is the Christianity that I understand, and these are the Christians whose teachings and actions I cannot match up together.

(Curtain falls)

2

THE COLORED FACES [1916] [18]

THE SCENE: The house of Yusuf Effendi al-Jammal, one of the leading Syrian merchants of New York

THE TIME: A cold, winter night

THE CAST: Yusuf Effendi al-Jammal

His wife, Miriam

Farid Effendi Ghantous, a journalist

Doctor Suleiman Beitar

Anis Effendi Farahat,
    a merchant and a writer

Miss Warda al-Azar

Father Ne'matallah Bakhous, a priest

Hannah al-Bashawati, a maidservant

And one other person

The curtains open on a large room, warm and with expensive furniture, but with mismatched colors and a fashion that suggests the wealth of the master of the house but at the same time the poor taste of its mistress. Guests sit comfortably and contentedly talking about the war and its outcomes, and amid

---

[18] Al-Qawwal notes that this play appeared in *As-Sayeh* [The Tourist], April 20, 1916, and is copied from *Aqidat Gibran* [The Doctrine of Gibran], pages 262-271.

their voices, the sound of Father Ne'matallah Bakhous' hookah rises from time to time. The doorbell rings, and a moment later, Miss Warda al-Azar enters with an English newspaper in her hand.

Miss Warda: Good evening!

All (rising): Good evening.

Mrs. Miriam al-Jammal: Welcome.

Miss Warda (She shakes hands with each person present, sits in the center of the room, and says, addressing all of them): Have you read what is in *The Sun* newspaper this evening?

Yusuf al-Jammal: What's the news? Is there anything about the war?

Miss Warda: No, no, nothing new about the war, but listen to this report. (She opens the newspaper and reads in a calm voice and an accent that shows her skill in the language of the country. She reads what translates as): "In honor of Syrian Salim Murjani, Mrs. Jean Hamilton held a party to which she invited the most renowned American authors and the greatest masters of fine arts. At the end of the celebration, Mr. Murjani stood up and gave a grand speech, speaking of Middle Eastern art and about the ideologies, ambitions, and creeds that at this time manipulate his country, Syria. He then read a poem he wrote in English, whose meaning and structure demonstrate a marvelous ability and vast imagination. The poem greatly impressed the guests at the party. We will publish Mr. Murjani's speech and poem in the Sunday edition

24

of this newspaper because we are also admirers of this Middle Eastern genius," etc., etc.

Doctor Beitar (yawning): I don't see anything important in this report! I know Salim Murjani very well. He is a young author. What English newspapers publish about him is not any different from what they write on lots of topics. American newspapers lie very much, miss, and in this arena they are even lower than Syrian newspapers.

Anis Farahat: That is the absolute truth. Don't you remember what the American news-papers said about Fathalla Shimon—that he is one of the princes and will marry a wealthy American? We all know who Fathalla Shimon is. As for that rich American, she is a woman of forty-five, and her father is a farmer in one of the western states.

I know him well—very well, actually. I have met him and spoken with him many times. In fact, we have met several times by coincidence in the same hotels and restaurants. He is a bright young man but with empty dreams. He thinks he can keep up with both sides in their arts and literature.

Father Ne'matallah Bakhous: I don't know Salim Murjani in person, and I don't want to. But I have heard a lot about him, and I have read some articles that suggest he is one of those infidel atheists who think they've made a gigantic accomplishment when they throw the church and its people along with the stones of their ignorance and disbelief.

Do any of you think that a young Lebanese man with morals and principles like these can ever succeed in achieving anything in this great country?

Yusuf al-Jammal: You've hit the nail on the head, Father. Salim Murjani is one of those arrogant young men who delude themselves into thinking that they will change the face of the Earth (smiles wickedly).

Remember the tale of the grasshopper and the ant—the one when the grasshopper went to the ant in winter and asked for some food? The ant asked the grasshopper, "What were you doing at harvest time?"

"Singing songs," he replied. (Everyone laughs except Miss Warda al-Azar.)

Doctor Beitar: How many mad lunatics there are among the Syrians! And how many of them concern themselves with things of no benefit to themselves or anyone else! What's worse is that every time a lunatic of this type appears among us, our newspapers move heaven and earth for him. American newspapers are well-known to be "yellow journalism," with a marked tendency to magnify trivial matters. In one of the Arabic newspapers, I once read a remark about Murjani that made me cancel my subscription to that newspaper. It didn't just call him an author and an artistic writer but made things worse by calling him "the Syrian genius." (Signs of anger show on the doctor's face. Then he raises his voice and adds:)

Flattery that reaches this level is actually a sort of mockery. If we call Salim Murjani a genius, what then should we call Sheik Ibrahim al-Yazji, scholar Abdullah al-Bustani, and the late Said al-Shartuni? I am not off track, and I am not exaggerating. I am in fact giving each person his due. If I had been the owner of the so-and-so newspaper, or the editor of the so-and-so newspaper—the nature of which is well-known to Syrians—my newspaper would have thousands of subscribers.

Honor, my friends, cannot be bought or sold. I would rather leave journalism and its trade altogether than begin to flatter this or that person. As for American newspapers, they are like prostitutes who solicit at street corners. And what did this Murjani ever do to be called a genius?

Yusuf al-Jammal: If Murjani were a genius, what would as-Sam'ani, Archbishop al-Zoghbi, or the priest al-Entalyasi be? I met this Murjani not long ago, and I asked him some questions about history. I found that he knew nothing. Then I asked him about the introduction to his last book. He muttered some words that I can't recall. Do we call a person of such a nature a genius? Oh dear God, there would be so many Syrian geniuses!

Anis Farahat: What greatly annoys and disgusts me is that our fellow, Murjani, fancies that if he lets his hair grow, carries a walking stick, and wears odd clothes, then he will gain people's respect and trust, the way the Western authors and scientists do.

Mrs. al-Jammal (addressing Father Ne'matallah Bakhous): The coals have died, Reverend. Let me refresh the hookah for you.

Father Ne'matallah Bakhous: No, no, my lady. I have smoked quite a bit. But as you wish.

Mrs. al-Jammal (calling the servant with a loud voice): Hannah, refresh the hookah for our Father, and bring us coffee.

(Hannah, the servant, enters the room. She is a woman in her fifties with broad and dignified features, and there is a look in her eyes that speaks silently of an inner grief caused by a longing for her homeland. After reading the faces of the guests, she takes Father Ne'matallah Bakhous' hookah and leaves the room.)

Miss Warda (turning to Miriam al-Jammal): Who is this servant? I've never seen her before.

Mrs. al-Jammal: A poor woman we hired two days ago to serve us. She is, as you see, an old lady, and she cannot serve very well, but we keep her as an act of kindness.

Miss Warda: In the lines of her face, I saw something that stirred my emotions and made my memories roam for a minute over the hills of Lebanon and its valleys. Who knows, it might be that this poor woman has an emotional story.

(The guests return to their last topic of conversation.)

Doctor Beitar: The goblet is lost to the Syrians, and none of them can distinguish between gold and ash.[19] Whoever graduates from a medical school is now called a doctor, and whoever composes poems is now called a poet. Were it not for this great fallacy, we wouldn't have those among us who say that Salim al-Murjani is a genius. In fact, no one would even mention his name. The goblet is lost, and with most of us blind, how will we find it?

(Miss Warda buries her face in her hands and heaves a deep sigh. She then looks at the guests. Her lips tremble slightly as though she has something to say, but she holds herself back in fear of sounding extreme.)

The Journalist, Farid Ghantous (addressing Miss Warda): Why are you so quiet, Miss Warda? You read the news to us and then became silent. You have not shared your opinion about Salim al-Murjani.

Miss Warda: I didn't voice my opinion because I find silence better than speaking.

Anis Farahat: You must have an opinion about Murjani. It clearly shows in the way you read *The Sun* article with a tone of joy and admiration.

Father Ne'matallah Bakhous: Yes, Miss Warda. Do share your opinion.

---

[19] "The goblet is lost" is an Arabic expression meaning that the people are blind. It comes from the popular Turkish baths in which bathers use a metal *taseh* (bowl-shaped goblet) to pour water on themselves. Should the goblet become lost, the bathers might be left covered in soap and unable to see.

Miss Warda (places her palms again over her eyes and then stares at the guests with eyes open wide. In a voice that reveals her agitation, she says): I do have an opinion, gentlemen. I have many opinions about Salim al-Murjani and every young man like him. I have an opinion—in fact many opinions—about all young men who leave the embrace of their mother, Syria, and go to Egypt, France, England, Brazil, or the United States and build monuments of artistic and literary glory for themselves and their homeland. I have many thoughts, but do my thoughts have a place on this stage? What can I say about Salim al-Murjani and all the ones like him now that you have given them their due compliment and praise?

The Sun mentions that Mrs. Hamilton held a party for Salim al-Murjani, and as you know, Mrs. Hamilton is an American. Nothing connects her with Murjani but a literary bond and her enthusiasm and great concern for literature and writers. You had doubts about this news because Murjani is a Syrian like you and in his veins flows the same blood as yours.

Why would Americans honor a Middle Eastern author? Is it for the beauty of his eyes, or for his lengthy hair, or for his foreign accent? Are they going to respect him because he was born among the barren valleys of Lebanon, or for being a descendent of the ancient prophets of Syria, or because he represents the majestic

Ottoman state? No, Americans don't care about such things, but they have a vision that selects foreigners who have an enlightened soul or those who have accomplished noble work, and they lay them on an altar of honor and encouragement. Americans are a very alive nation, and they know that a nation becomes known for its geniuses. They don't discriminate between a genius coming from Paris and a genius from the heart of Africa. They give all who are superior their due, something you yourselves cannot do.

When I read the report in *The Sun* to you, your faces grew pale and your tongues got confused, as though I had brought you joyous news about your worst enemy. If there were an American sitting with us who understood our language, he would think that Salim al-Murjani had strangled your parents with his own hands just before his brilliance led him to Mrs. Hamilton's celebration last night.

Doctor Beitar called the American newspaper "yellow journalism" just because it admired his fellow citizen. Anis Effendi Farahat said he knows Salim al-Murjani, and since he knows him fully, he concludes that Salim can't keep up with the West in its arts and literature. The esteemed Father said that nothing great could be expected of al-Murjani because he throws the church and its people along with the stones of his own ignorance and disbelief. Yusuf Effendi al-Jammal takes al-Murjani to be a grasshopper, but he didn't mention who the ant is!

This is what you said, gentlemen, about a young man whose brilliance makes him a golden chain that connects the stagnant Syrian nation to the sophisticated West. That's what you say about a man who makes the elite of this country take note of our presence among them. That's what you say about a burning flame that God kindled in Syria, which destiny carried to the lands of immigration.

If that is what you say, then what can I say? Shall I say that envy is a vile characteristic in Syrians? Shall I say that feelings of national pride have died in the souls of Syrians? Shall I say that our community does not perceive the value of an individual if he is Syrian? Shall I say that it is your duty and the duty of all Syrians to honor al-Murjani and all talented persons among us, just as Westerners honor their talented individuals? Shall I say that the Syrian trend has generally fallen towards material gain, to the point that no desire remains in their being for anything higher? Shall I say that the Turkish rule has killed the noble feelings of your hearts?

No, I respect you as individuals, and at the same time, I respect myself and would not say anything of that sort. But I hope that the principles that led to the awakening of the Western nations will awaken in the souls of your children or your grandchildren—that moral awakening which transformed their lives into an everlasting wedding on the stage of existence, while in the meantime, we, the Middle Easterners, are at a funeral drenched in tears and groaning.

I am a woman, and the voice of women is not heard among Easterners. If it had been heard, I would tonight have made you understand things you need to understand. Even more, I am an unmarried woman, and your old traditions say that an unmarried girl must remain silent as tombs and idle as stones. (Miss Warda turns her head away and heaves the sigh of a bereaved person. The guests look at her puzzled. Then some of them start laughing.)

Doctor Beitar: It appears to me, Miss Warda, that there are reasons that lead you to take great interest in Salim al-Murjani.

Anis Farahat (winks at Doctor Beitar and says): Miss Warda must be one of those who are very interested in authors....

Father Ne'matallah Bakhous: Despite the offensive criticism that Miss Warda has directed towards us, I respect her out of respect for her father and uncle.

Miss Warda: Thank you, Father. I hope that the future will lead you to respect me for myself. I don't know Salim al-Murjani, and I don't care to know him in person. I read his writings, and that is enough. But let's suppose that I were interested in him personally. Would my interest be a reason for what you said about him tonight? Isn't there a faculty that allows

Syrians to separate what is personal from what is general? A man with sight admires the light of day even though he knows that the sun was not created for him personally. A sighted man loves the light of the sun, and a blind man appreciates and seeks its warmth, but what can we say about a blind man who lives at the North Pole!

Farid Effendi Ghantous: Dear God, what's all this—a blind man and the North Pole!

Doctor Beitar: And the cause of all this is a deranged young man with empty dreams!

Anis Farahat: The young lady glares at us in disdain because we don't share her admiration for a fraudulent nobody! (Just at this moment, the bell rings, and a brief silence falls.)

Yusuf al-Jammal (opens the door and asks in English): Who are you looking for, and what do you want?

A Young Man (standing at the door, answers in Arabic:) I am sorry to bother you, sir. I am in search of a woman who recently came from the homeland. I was told that she is working in your household.

Yusuf al-Jammal: Who is this woman?

The Young Man: Her name is Hannah al-Bashawati, sir, and she is from the north of Lebanon.

Yusuf al-Jammal: A woman entered our service two days ago, and her name is um-Naufal.

The Young Man: That's her, sir! That's her! Would you do me a great favor and tell her that Salim al-Murjani wants to meet her? (Before the young man even finishes saying his name, the faces of the guests change and their eyes flare as if a meteor had crashed right in the middle of the room.)

Yusuf al-Jammal (with cheer): Please come in, Murjani Effendi.

Anis Farahat (leaves his seat and walks to the door, saying): Welcome, Salim! What brings you to Brooklyn?

(Salim al-Murjani enters the room, removes his hat, and bows to greet the guests. They all rise, and the looks on their faces speak silently of devils and demons racing in their hearts. But Miss Warda's face looks overjoyed, and she senses that something unexpected is about to happen. She gazes at al-Murjani's face for a moment and then turns to look at each of the guests.)

Yusuf al-Jammal: Allow me, Salim Effendi, to introduce you to the Reverend Father Ne'matallah Bakhous....

Father Ne'matallah Bakhous: It's an honor. It's an honor.

Yusuf al-Jammal: And this is Doctor Suleiman Effendi al-Beitar, Mr. Farid Effendi Ghantous, and Mr. Anis Farahat. And allow me, Effendi, to introduce you to my wife, Mrs. Jammal.

All (in different voices): We are honored. We are honored. (Miss Warda remains standing, and Salim al-Murjani looks at her and says:)

Salim al-Murjani: I have not had the pleasure of being introduced to the lady here.

Mrs. al-Jammal: Pardon me. Pardon me, Effendi. Allow me to introduce you to Miss Warda al-Azar, one of the well-known and most brilliant writers.

Salim al-Murjani (bows before Miss Warda, saying): I am honored to meet you.

Miss Warda: It is my good fortune and honor to meet you, Murjani Effendi, especially on this particular night.

(Everyone takes their seats. After some meaningless greetings and small talk, Salim al-Murjani addresses the master of the house:)

Salim al-Murjani: I have been searching for Hannah al-Bashawati since six o'clock, and after some time, one of the Syrians led me to your house. I have a letter and a bank draft from Brazil bearing her name. So, please, Mr. Jammal Effendi, call for her so I can meet her.

Mrs. al-Jammal (calling loudly): Um-Naufal! Um-Naufal![20] Come here a minute.

Hannah al-Bashawati (enters the hall; Salim al-Murjani stands, and the moment she lays her eyes on him, she screams from the bottom of her heart, saying): Oh my dearest Salim. (Tears shimmer in her eyes, and she continues:) You fill my heart. I cannot believe this is you! I asked about you when I arrived, and they said you were in Boston. Oh, how sweet it is to look at your face.

---

[20] There are several ways of respectfully addressing people in Arabic. One is by their own name, and the other is by the name of their first male son. Thus, her name is Hannah al-Bashawati, but a respectful alternative is um-Naufal, meaning mother of Naufal.

You've made me forget my feelings of separation and the aching of my heart. (She approaches him, hugs and kisses him, and then they sit down.)

Salim al-Murjani: Um-Naufal, I have a letter and a bank draft from Brazil in your name. (He takes a large envelope from his pocket and places it in the hands of Hannah al-Bashawati.)

(Hannah al-Bashawati opens it, and after reading the letter and looking at the draft, she buries her face in her hands and sobs.)

(Salim al-Murjani approaches her and gently places his hand on her shoulder. He leans with care and says): We are all immigrants separated from our homeland, um-Naufal, and such separation grieves the heart but doesn't break it. It makes it grow. God will bring us all back together in our homeland, and we will live again as we used to.

Hannah al-Bashawati: Oh, how I miss the old days! What a great difference there is between yesterday and today! Who would have believed that the wife of Khalil al-Bashawati would become a servant in a foreign land?

Salim al-Murjani: We are all servants, um-Naufal. We are all servants, and those who do not serve deserve neither the light of day nor the repose of the night.

(Hannah al-Bashawati begins to cry again, to the point that she can no longer speak. Mrs. Miriam al-Jammal stands up, helps her out of the room, and returns a minute later.)

(Salim al-Murjani:) This woman was very well off, and she had a much-respected status in my hometown. She was very kind to my family in ways I will never forget. I would like so much to be helpful to her in some way.

Anis Farahat (trying to change the subject): How are you, Salim Effendi? I haven't seen you for a month or more. I asked about you many times and was told that you had disappeared among the Americans.

Doctor Beitar: We read an article about you tonight in *The Sun* newspaper, and it's a joy, Murjani Effendi, to hear such fine comments about our writers.

Father Ne'matallah Bakhous: The enthusiasm of Americans for writers is well known, especially when the author is someone like Murjani Effendi.

Farid Effendi Ghantous: I read a delightful article by you, Murjani Effendi, in one of the Egyptian magazines, and I can't tell you how impressed I was. I had intended to publish it in my own newspaper, were it not for my hope to have a new article by your ever-flowing pen.

Yusuf al-Jammal: What a marvelous coincidence brought you to us tonight, Salim Effendi. All the credit goes to um-Naufal.

Mrs. al-Jammal: I hope you will honor us again by having dinner with us next week.

Salim al-Murjani: I thank you, madam, for your generous hospitality. I have been away a long time from the people of my homeland, and all because of work. But whenever I see a Syrian, my heart races

38

and my soul rushes to him. I do hope to see you all very soon. (He stands to leave, but the master of the house stops him.)

Yusuf al-Jammal: Coffee is on the way, and the evening has just begun.

Salim al-Murjani (sits again): I will not argue with you, sir. It has been weeks since I've had a cup of Syrian coffee.

Anis Farahat: Murjani Effendi is very fond of coffee, and he drinks it day and night.

Doctor Beitar: Coffee stimulates talent, but Murjani Effendi's talent needs no stimulation.

Mrs. al-Jammal (calling loudly): Um-Naufal, bring the coffee!

Um-Naufal's voice (coming from the kitchen): Yes, Mrs. Miriam.

Father Ne'matallah Bakhous (addressing Miss Warda): Why are you so quiet, Miss Warda?

Miss Warda: I have nothing to say in your presence, Reverend. You are the speakers, and people like me should listen. If fortune had brought Murjani Effendi to this house at the beginning of this evening, I would not have uttered a word. And we must not forget, Reverend, that it is considered impolite among Syrians for an unmarried woman to speak in the presence of men. But I am pleased to see you all so cheerful upon meeting Murjani Effendi, and as Hamlet said before he died, "The rest is silence."

Doctor Beitar: Spare us, Miss Warda, these obscurities.

Miss Warda: Oh, how adept we are at devoting time to obscurities and non-obscurities. I would like to say something now about obscurities, but I want Murjani Effendi to enjoy his cup of coffee. Do you remember the words of the poet, "The frog said words understood by the wise: 'There is water in my mouth. Would anyone speak with water in their mouth?'"[21]

Salim al-Murjani: It looks like I came at a time when you were having a private conversation, and I interrupted you.

Yusuf al-Jammal: No, no, sir, we were just talking generally.

Father Ne'matallah Bakhous: Winter nights are long, and we pass them conversing about different topics for amusement.

Salim al-Murjani: Your discussion must have been very pleasant. I sense from what Miss Warda said about Hamlet and the frog, and how I should enjoy my cup of coffee, what confirms to me that your conversation is not for a stranger like me.

(Hannah enters with a cup of coffee on a tray, which Murjani takes while Hannah looks at him with excitement and affection.)

(Yusuf al-Jammal offers a cigarette to al-Murjani, who lights it and begins to smoke between sips of coffee. Once finished, he stands up, intending to leave, and all rise in respect for him. After shaking hands with each of them, he says good-bye to um-Naufal and

---

[21] The quote refers to an Arabic saying and implies that there are times when it is best to keep silent.

promises to meet with her soon. He thanks his host and hostess and then leaves the room.)

(The men remain silent until the stillness of the night absorbs the sound of Salim al-Murjani's footsteps. They then look quietly at each other as if the hands of some unseen spirit were clutching their necks, except for Miss Warda al-Azar, who bears a smile of a thousand meanings. After a silence that sounds like the wails of the abyss and the death rattles of a man in his last gasp, Miss Warda al-Azar stands, walks to the door, and says:)

Miss Warda: There is no doubt that you will spend the rest of the evening quietly, remorsefully, and in repentance. Yes, gentlemen, for you now, silence is better than speaking. But if you must talk, let it be about matters that have to do with loyalty and freedom of thought.

The last hour of this evening has been one of the best, deepest, and most noble hours of my life, because it drew before my eyes an image of Syrians as a group, and it clarified for me the reasons that made Syrians drag their chains from Babylon to Memphis, to Baghdad, and to Istanbul. This last hour has shown me the Syrians' ability to fabricate and distort, and at the same time their skill in creating ironies with different features.

Yes, gentlemen, we all have many faces. In the blue hour, we wear blue faces, in the yellow hour, we wear yellow faces, and in the red hour, we wear red faces. So on and so forth to the end of the color spectrum. Good evening, gentlemen.

(Miss Warda al-Azar leaves, closing the door behind her with strength and force, like someone escaping from hell. The others remain silent, staring at the ceiling as though they see a horrifying demon holding a notebook in his hand, writing down everything they had said about Salim al-Murjani before the night had brought him to them.)

(Curtain falls)

3

BETWEEN NIGHT AND MORNING [1918] [22]

THE SCENE: A dark, narrow, prison dungeon in Beirut's central government district, located in Tower Square

THE TIME: About midnight on the 9th of October

THE CAST: Yusuf Karamah, a poet

                   Saleem Ballan, a prominent Christian

                   Ali Rahman, a prominent Muslim

                   Sharaf-Addeen al-Horani,

                         a prominent Druze

                   Musa Hayeem, a Jewish merchant

Musa Hayeem and Sharaf-Addeen al-Horani are both sleeping in different corners of the dungeon. Saleem Ballan is resting his head on his forearm. Ali Rahman is sitting on a wooden chair. Yusuf Karamah is pacing aimlessly back and forth across the cell and stops from time to time, gazing towards the small opening through which the starlight enters.

---

[22] Al-Qawwal notes that this play was published in *As-Sayeh,* January 16, 1919, according to John Dayeh in *Aqidat Gibran,* pages 293-297. [Allied forces reached Beirut on October 8, 1918, and Gibran must have written the play shortly thereafter.]

Musa Hayeem (talking in his sleep): Two hundred plus two hundred is four hundred. Four hundred plus three hundred is seven hundred. Seven hundred plus two hundred is nine hundred. Nine hundred plus five hundred is one thousand four hundred in gold. They took it! They took it from me! They took it. Oh no, no!

Yusuf Karamah: I wish I could get some sleep like he does. I wish I could shut my eyes to this hell for even one minute and open them in a world far away from this one!

Ali Rahman (in a tone of kindness): I've noticed that you haven't slept for a week, my brother, and I don't know how you can stand without sleep. Lay down, brother. Lay down on these wooden boards and sleep, even if only for an hour. Don't you see that the longer you stay continuously awake, the closer it drives you to a slow suicide?

Yusuf Karamah: No, I don't want to commit suicide in this filthy den. My life has seen enough humiliation. If my life had any value, they wouldn't have kept me alive. If it had any value, they would have hanged it with a rope as they did with the lives of my friends and brothers. No, I was not worthy of the honor of death with the others who died. I wasn't worth the nobility of the gallows!

Ali Rahman: Calm down. Don't think about yesterday. We have to survive until tomorrow, because tomorrow is in the hands of God, and God is generous and merciful.

Yusuf Karamah: How can I stop my thoughts from rushing through my head? How can I forget yesterday? The hand of yesterday holds tightly the conscience of today. Yesterday is a parade of grey shadows floating in the space of this prison, a carousel of ghosts whirling around my head, whispering in my ears the names of my comrades, the names of my martyred brothers, the names of the people who were left hanging between heaven and earth.

Ali Rahman (standing up in anger): I swear by God who holds my soul in His hand that one day our sons will avenge us. There will be men among the new generation who will avenge our blood. They will appear as a giant from the Arabian Peninsula, proud of his strength, marching and smashing tyrants and oppressors beneath his feet.

Sharaf-Addeen al-Horani (wakes up, rubbing his eyes with his fingers, and addresses Ali Rahman, saying): You are daydreaming an empty dream. Arabs, sir, are a people lost between the sands and the mountains of the Arabian Peninsula. It is foolishness to expect anything great from them. The future of Syria depends on the stance of the powerful and the just British state, and if England does not occupy Syria, then Syria will be finished.

Saleem Ballan: Do you want the arrogant and pretentious England to occupy a country whose people worship France? And would we accept any nation but France to protect and rule us? I tell you, France is the cradle of freedom and the mother of civilization, and if her tricolored flag does not fly above the plains and mountains of Syria, then Syria shall be without hope or future.

Musa Hayeem (talking in his sleep): Two hundred and two hundred is four hundred. Four hundred and three hundred is seven hundred. They took it! They took it! Oh no! They took it!

Yusuf Karamah (stands in the middle of the room, raising his arms): Oh, how great is your calamity, Syria! The souls of your sons do not flow through your frail body but through the bodies of other nations. Their hearts abandoned you, and their thoughts moved away from you. O Syria, Syria, the widow of the generations and the bereaved of the ages. O Syria, land of misfortunes, the bodies of your sons are still in your arms, but their hearts are far away from you. One heart wanders in the Arabian Peninsula, another walks the streets of London, another flutters and flies over the palaces of Paris, and one counts coins in its sleep. O Syria, you are a mother of no children!

(Addressing his companions:) Listen, you prisoners confined in a prison within a prison within a prison. Syria is not for the Arabs, and neither for the English, the French, nor the Jews. Syria is for you and me. Your bodies that are made of Syria's soil are for Syria. Your souls that were raised under Syria's sky are for Syria—not for any other country under the sun.

God knows that I love Arabs, and I am eager to see their glory restored. But I am Syrian, and I want a Syrian glory for Syria. God knows I respect the justice of England, and I admire its determination. But I am Syrian, and I want Syrian justice and determination for Syria. God knows, and you all know too, that my feelings of gratefulness to France have led me to this prison. But regardless of my love for that noble nation, which walks ahead of all nations on Earth towards disentangled rights and absolute freedom, I am Syrian, and I want Syrian rights and Syrian freedom for Syria.

Ali Rahman: My brother, you are a poet expressing your imagination with beautiful words, but poetry is a different matter.

Sharaf-Addeen: You do well, Ali Effendi, to call him a poet, praise be to God, because poets don't rule Britain.

Saleem Ballan: And who said that people of imagination rule France?

Musa Hayeem (in his sleep): Two hundred and two hundred is four hundred. Four hundred and three hundred is seven hundred. They took it in gold and silver!

Yusuf Karamah: Yes, a poet, not a politician, and I don't want to be a politician. I love my country and its people, and that is all I want to know about politics. I love my nation because it is weak, wronged, and oppressed. If my country were strong and great, I would have left its love and become occupied with the ghosts and dreams of my soul. I love the people of my country because they are lost and confused, and they fear the future by hating the past. They fear the days ahead even if they smile at them. But if the people of my country were strong, united, and in agreement, I would forget them and their needs and ambitions, and I would explore the hidden secrets of life. I love my country and its people, and love has eyes that see what politics cannot see, and ears that hear what philosophy cannot apprehend.

Sharaf-Addeen: I love Syria too, and no one can doubt that, but it is my love for Syria that makes me eager for that day when Syria becomes a living organ in the body of the great British Empire.

Saleem Ballan: He who loves Syria must also love the people who love her. Is there any nation that cares for Syria the way the French nation does? Since the time of the Crusaders, France has watched over our country with a vigilant eye, and as I see it, anyone who doesn't love France as much as he loves Syria is ungrateful.

Ali Rahman: I don't discredit anyone's respect for England, and I'm not steering anyone away from his love for France, but I ask you, what relationship connects the East with the West other than colonial ambitions? The East and the West are two separate worlds, and no bond can unite them, nor can any philosophy or policy bring them closer. So I say that the Syrians and Arabs must be one kingdom and one people, for we share the same history and language, and our country is part of theirs.

Musa Hayeem (while sleeping): Two hundred and two hundred is four hundred...four hundred and three hundred is seven hundred...they took it...they took it in gold and silver...!

Yusuf Karamah (buries his face in his hands, then raises his head and cries): O Babel, o Babel, you are the city of separation! Did the shadow of God abandon you and leave you like ruins in a desert? O Babel, o Babel, you are a land of disagreement and feud! Did you, in your dreams, build a tower that reaches the sky, arousing the anger of God, who confounded your tongue and scattered your men all over the face of the Earth? O Babel, o Babel, you are a city with no people! Will your sons ever return to rebuild your walls and temples? Will God pass by again and free you from your humiliation? O Babel, o Babel, a city with houses of pain, streets of misfortune, and rivers of tears! O Babel, o Babel, you are the city of my heart!

(Yusuf stops speaking, as if the torment has choked him. He then throws himself on the wooden boards, exhausted. A deep silence then descends, like that of a terrifying graveyard. Half an hour later, behind the curtains of silence, some faint noises are heard coming from the Tower Square beyond the prison walls.)

***

Sound of a Child: Mother, I'm hungry, hungry. Give me a piece of bread. Just give me a little bite. I'm hungry, hungry.

Sound of a Woman: Sleep, my son. Sleep until morning. When dawn comes, God will send us bread, and we will all eat.

Sound of a Man: I have called for God until my throat became sore. God has died. God has died of hunger. If God were alive, none of his servants would have died like dogs in alleyways.

Sound of the Woman: Forgive him, Lord. He doesn't know what he's saying.

Sound of the Child (cheered): Mother, look! Look at that table of food, the banquet table! It is full of bread, meat, poultry, and fish. Look at the bowls of honey, cheese, and yoghurt. Look at it, Mother. Reach out and give me, give me, give me. Ah, ah!

Sound of the Woman (After a moment of silence, she wails in pain): He's dead! My son has died. The last of my sons has died. Oh Lord, look at me.

Sound of the Man: Your son died while you were calling to God. I told you, God has died of hunger.

Sound of the Woman (with conviction): God is alive. Thank you, Lord, for you took my son to a place where there is neither thirst nor hunger. Oh Lord, have mercy on all mothers this night.

***

Yusuf Karamah (rises in anger and beats on the wall with his hands): My homeland, homeland of pain, you said that you are

50

a heritage for your sons, but is there anyone left under the sun who could inherit you, an empty land with nothing but the corpses...?

I can hear the creaking sound of Death's feet as he walks through the streets of the sleeping city. I see him with his scythe, harvesting the souls of my brothers.

O Syria, you are the land where the routes of the conquerors meet. Will I live to see a new conqueror? Let the conqueror come. If the pockets of his soldiers are full of bread, let him come, for he may become a brother of mine who protects me and a sister whose voice I hear....

Oh, how selfish I am! I want to stay alive to see the face of a brother and a sister, but if my life had value, they would not have left it to me. If my life were of value, they would have hanged it with a rope, with those who were strung up with the look of defeat on their faces. (He looks around him and finds that all of his companions have fallen asleep. He crosses his arms over his chest and paces back and forth across the gloomy room.)

IN THE MORNING

(Yusuf Karamah is still pacing nervously in the middle of the cell, and his companions are still sleeping. He hears a commotion outside the prison, followed by gunshots and screams from every direction. Several minutes later, he hears the sound of jubilation and singing.)

(Yusuf Karamah, shouting as loudly as he can): Wake up! Wake up quickly, all you sleepers! Get up and listen. The viper has left and removed its shadow from this city! (The prisoners get up quickly, wondering, shouting, crying, laughing, as if they have gone mad.)

(Voices from outside.)

(Yusuf Karamah:) The soldiers of the allies have filled the city—England's army, France's armored vehicles, India's troops, Italians, and French. Praise be to God! All praise be to God! We have been saved!

(Hardly a moment passes before the door of the prison opens. Light fills the dark, musty room. Overjoyed, Musa Hayeem leaves, followed by Sharaf-Addeen al-Horani, Saleem Ballan, and Ali Rahman. Yusuf remains standing in the middle of the room, gazing at the sunlight passing through the entrance of the prison. He walks slowly towards the door, saying to himself:)

Oh Lord, let my stepping outside this prison be to real freedom. Oh Lord, don't let me fly with my wings spread open over a garden full of hunters. You didn't create my life to be a sacrifice on the altar of justice and freedom, so make of it an incense if you wish.

(Curtain falls)

4

AL-SULBAN [1920] [23]

THE SCENE: The home of Yusuf Masarrah in Beirut

THE TIME: An autumn night in 1901

THE CAST: Bulus al-Sulban,
      an author and a musician

      Yusuf Masarrah,
      an author and a man of letters

      Miss Helanah Masarrah,
      Yusuf's sister

      Salim Mu'awad,
      a poet and an oud player

      Khalil Beik Tamer, a government clerk

The curtains open on an elegant room in Yusuf Masarrah's home, filled with books and papers. Khalil Beik Tamer is smoking a hookah, Miss Helanah is knitting, and Yusuf Masarrah is smoking a cigarette.

Khalil Beik (addressing Yusuf Masarrah): I read your article today about fine arts and their influence on morals. I liked it very much. If it weren't for the Western

---

[23] *Al-Sulban* appeared in Gibran's book, *Al-A'waseif* (The Storms, or Tempests), published by Dar al-Hilal, Cairo, in 1920. It first appeared in English in a translation by Anthony R. Ferris entitled *Assilban*, in the Gibran collection, *Spiritual Sayings* (New York: Citadel Press, 1962).

flavor it has, it would have been the best article written on this subject. I'm one of those, Masarrah Effendi, who consider the influence of Western literature on our language as a harmful thing.

Yusuf Masarrah (smiling): You may be right, my friend, but by wearing Western clothing, eating with Western utensils, and sitting on Western chairs, you contradict yourself. Even more, you prefer reading Western books over Arabic ones.

Khalil Beik: Such superficial things have no relationship whatsoever with literature and the arts.

Yusuf Masarrah: Ah, but there is a vital relationship. If you delve just a little into the subject, you will find that the arts go hand in hand with our habits, fashions, and social and religious traditions. In fact, they accompany every feature of our social lives.

Khalil Beik: I am a Middle Eastern man, and I shall remain so for the rest of my life, and in spite of some European characteristics I have, I hope that Arabic literature will remain pure and free of all foreign influences.

Yusuf Masarrah: Then are you wishing for the death of the Arabic language and literature?

Khalil Beik: How is that?

Yusuf Masarrah: Older nations that fail to benefit from the fruits of modern ones face a literary death and become morally extinct.

Khalil Beik: What you say requires proof.

Yusuf Masarrah: I have a thousand and one proofs. (At this moment, Bulus al-Sulban and Salim Mu'awad enter. The others stand in respect.)

Welcome brothers. (Addressing al-Sulban:) Warm welcome to you, Syria's nightingale. (Miss Helanah looks at al-Sulban with a blush on her cheeks and signs of happiness on her face.)

Salim Mu'awad: For heaven's sake, Yusuf, don't pay Bulus even one compliment.

Yusuf Masarrah: And why is that?

Salim Mu'awad (half joking): Because he doesn't deserve any honoring, flattering, or praising, because he is an odd fellow with very strange ways and morals, and because he's mad.

Bulus al-Sulban (addressing Mu'awad): Did I bring you along so you would disclose my flaws and reveal my morals?

Miss Helanah: I wonder what happened. Have you discovered, Salim Effendi, some new flaws in Bulus' behavior?

Salim Mu'awad: His old flaws will remain new until he dies, gets buried, and his bones turn to dust.

Yusuf Masarrah: Tell us, what happened? Tell us the whole story from beginning to end.

Salim Mu'awad (addressing al-Sulban): Will you allow me to speak of your crimes, Bulus, or do you want to confess them yourself?

Bulus al-Sulban: I want you to be as silent as a cemetery and as still as an old woman's heart.

Salim Mu'awad: Then I will speak.

Bulus al-Sulban: It appears that you are determined to ruin my evening.

Salim Mu'awad: No, I want to put your story before these friendly people to consider your case.

Miss Helanah (addressing Mu'awad): Speak up and tell us what happened. (To al-Sulban:) It could be that the crime Salim wants to reveal is actually one of your virtues.

Bulus al-Sulban: I committed neither crime nor virtue. The matter that our friend wants to tell you about doesn't deserve to be mentioned, and besides, I don't want you to waste the evening talking about me.

Miss Helanah: All right then, let's hear the news!

Salim Mu'awad (lights a cigarette and sits beside Yusuf Masarrah): You've all heard, of course, of the marriage of Jalal Pasha's son, and you know that last night the groom's father hosted a tarab[24] and invited all the city notables and leaders. (Pointing to Bulus:) He also invited this evil man, and me, for the simple reason that people see me as Bulus' shadow who goes wherever he goes and stands wherever he stands, and because he—may God protect and save him—doesn't like to sing except to the sounds of my oud.

Well, we arrived late at Jalal Pasha's house, and our Bulus, just like a king, is always late. There we found the

---

[24] A *tarab* is a musical party at which the songs are based on classical Arabic poems with many vocal solos. It is known for its emotional and even trance-like fervor.

governor, the archbishop, virtuous and pretty ladies, authors, poets, wealthy men, and leaders. We sat between incense burners and wine goblets, and people looked at Bulus as if looking at an angel that had just descended from the sky.

Women started serving him glasses of wine, trays of nuts, and flower bouquets, just like the women of Athens would do when a hero returned from war. In brief, our Bulus was, at the beginning of the evening, a subject of ovation and glorification.

I took my oud and played a first, second, then third melody. Bulus opened his sacred lips and sang a verse, just one single verse, of ibn al-Farid's poem, "Everyone but me finds comfort in consolation, and in love, everyone but me is a traitor." People listened attentively and craned their necks as though al-Musilli had emerged from behind the clouds of eternity to whisper some magical and celestial tune in their ears. Then Bulus was silent. The guests thought he would continue singing after another glass of arak,[25] but Bulus remained quiet.

Bulus al-Sulban (in a serious tone): Please stop at this point. I can't bear to listen to this useless talk, and I have no doubts that our friends find no pleasure in this meaningless babble either.

Yusuf Masarrah: By all means, let's hear the rest!

---

[25] Arak is a strong, anise-flavored liqueur, popular in the Middle East.

Bulus al-Sulban (rising from his seat): It's obvious that you prefer this pointless prattle rather than my presence among you. I fare you well.

Miss Helanah (looking at Bulus with a deep and meaningful look): Please sit, Bulus. Whatever the news might be, we are with you. (Bulus sits, with signs of impatience and forbearance on his face.)

Salim Mu'awad (continuing): As I was saying, Bulus, the sweet-scented and magnificent, recited a verse, just a single verse, of ibn al-Farid and then stopped. By this I mean that he let those poor, hungry people taste a single morsel of the divine food and then kicked the table away, broke its utensils and glasses, and sat in silence like the Sphinx on the sands of the Nile.

The ladies, one after the other, came to him and begged him with the sweetest of words to sing another song, while he apologized to them, saying, "I have a cold. My throat is sore." Then the notables and wealthy men came begging to him, humbling themselves before him. But he didn't soften or relent. Instead, he remained staunch, fixed, and rigid, as though God had replaced his heart with a granite rock and changed the melodies of his soul into mere flirtation and coquetry.

Then, around midnight, when the guests had become filled with painful despair, Jalal Pasha called him and took him to an adjacent room. He then placed a handful of dinars in his pocket and said, "Bulus Effendi, you can end our party with either joy or sorrow, so I hope you will accept this little gift, not as a reward but as a way to express my affection for you. So don't disappoint me or the guests."

But with that, Bulus stood up straight with pride on his face, threw the dinars onto a nearby chair, assumed the tone of a conquering king, and said, "You insult me, Jalal Pasha. No, you deprecate me. I did not come to your place to chant and sing and sell my breath for money. I came as one of the guests."

With that, Jalal Pasha lost his patience and his temper, and said some harsh words that made sensitive Bulus leave the house cursing and swearing. And I, poor me, took my oud and followed Bulus, leaving behind lovely faces, slender legs, good wines, and delicious food. Yes, I sacrificed all of that so as not to lose the friendship of this stubborn and obstinate one. I sacrificed all of that on the altar of this divine being, and still he hasn't thanked me, nor praised my courage, and not even acknowledged my loyalty and friendship.

Yusuf Masarrah (laughing): This is really a delicious tale. It should be written with needles on the eyelids![26]

---

[26] A reference to *The Arabian Nights*: "My story is of such marvel that if it were written with a needle on the corner of an eye, it would yet serve as a lesson to those who seek wisdom." Masarrah is implying that everyone should hear of this.

Salim Mu'awad: But I haven't reached the end of the story yet. The real joy is in the ending, that demonic ending which neither the Persian Ahriman nor the Shiva of the Indians has even dreamt of.

Bulus al-Sulban (addressing Miss Helanah): I have stayed here out of respect for you, and now please ask this frog to stop his croaking at this point.

Miss Helanah: Let him speak, Bulus! Whatever the end of the story, we are with you heart and soul.

Salim Mu'awad (lights another cigarette and continues): As I was saying, we left Jalal Pasha's house with Bulus swearing at the notables and the wealthy, while I was secretly swearing at him! And then.... Well, do you think that each of us just went to his own home? Do you think last night ended that way? Listen and be amazed!

You know that Habib Sa'ada's house is close to Jalal Pasha's house and is only a small garden away. And you know that Habib Sa'ada is fond of wine, melodies, and daydreams, and is among those who worship this divine being (pointing at Bulus). When we left Jalal Pasha's house, Bulus stood for a minute in the middle of the road, rubbing his forehead like some great leader pondering the conquest of an apostate kingdom. He then suddenly walked to Habib Sa'ada's house and rang the bell forcefully.

Habib Sa'ada appeared in his night-gown, rubbing his eyes, mumbling and yawning. But as soon as he saw Bulus' face, and me holding an oud under my arm, his features changed and his eyes sparkled as though heaven had opened before him! He cried out in joy and welcoming words, saying, "What brings you here in the wee hours of the night?"

Bulus answered, "We have come to celebrate the wedding of Jalal Pasha's son at your house."

Habib asked him, "Is the house of Jalal Pasha so small that you come to this little home?"

Bulus replied, "The walls of Jalal Pasha's house have no ears to hear the melodies of the oud and of song. That's why we have come to you. So bring a bottle of arak and a tray of meza,[27] and don't talk so much."

In short, we sat around the drinking table, and as soon as Bulus finished a glass or two of arak, he stood up and opened the windows that look out onto the Pashas' garden. He handed me the oud and said in a commanding voice, "This is your staff, Moses. Turn it into a snake, and let it swallow all the serpents of Egypt. Play a Nahawand,[28] and play it long and sweet."

Well, what can a servant do but obey? I took the oud and played a Nahawand, and Bulus turned his face towards Jalal Pasha's house and started singing in a loud voice. (Here

---

[27] Meza, or mezze, are Lebanese appetizers.
[28] Nahawand is a particular style of traditional Arabic music.

Salim stops talking for a minute. The look of humor fades from his face, and he says in a calm and serious tone:)

I have known Bulus for fifteen years. I have known him since we were boys at school. I have heard him sing in joy and in sorrow. I have heard him weep like a mourner, chant like a lover, and cheer like a winner. I have heard him whisper in the silence of night as the city and its people fall asleep. I have heard him from among the valleys of Lebanon and with the bells of distant churches filling the space with magic and majesty. Yes, I have heard him sing a thousand and one times, and I thought I knew the turmoils and tranquilities of his soul. But last night, when he turned his face towards Jalal Pasha's house, closed his eyes, and started singing, "Every day, I bemoan the love in my heart, and every time I bemoan, my love grows...."—when he sang out this verse, playing with its words as the wind plays with autumn leaves—I said to myself that "no, I know nothing of Bulus' soul but the skin, but now I have reached to the core. In the past, I never heard more than the singing of Bulus' tongue, but now I hear his heart and soul."

Bulus continued verse after verse, moving from song to song in such a way that I thought the space was filled with the souls of beloveds, hovering, whispering, calling, replaying the memories of the ancient past, and revealing people's dreams and yearnings that were long concealed by the night. Yes, gentlemen (pointing to Bulus), last night this man ascended the ladder of art until he reached the very planets, and it was a marvel that he didn't descend to Earth before dawn. He didn't stop singing until he had "trampled his enemies under his feet," as it's said in the Psalms.

When the guests of Jalal Pasha heard his voice coming from Habib Sa'ada's house, they crowded the windows and sat down, men and women, sighing after each part and each tune that came from his mouth. Some went out into the garden and stood under the trees, happy, tormented, and listening intently, in awe, baffled by this divine being who insults and humiliates them yet at the same time fills their hearts with a heavenly wine. Some were calling to him, imploring, begging, and wishing, while others were swearing and threatening.

And I heard from one of the guests that Jalal Pasha was roaring like a lion, going from room to room cursing al-Sulban, furious with those he had invited, especially those that had gone to the garden taking in their hands their glasses of arak and plates of delicacies. That is what happened last night.

Now, what do you say about this crazy genius? What do you say about the odd character of this man and his strange morals?

Khalil Beik: It's a very strange affair. As for what I
                 think of it, I'm an admirer of Bulus
                 Effendi's talents, and yet, with all due
                 respect, I would say that he was in
                 error last night. He could have sung
                 at Jalal Pasha's the same way he
                 did at Habib Sa'ada's house, and thus
                 answered the pleas of the people
                 with some of his artistic abilities.
                 (Addressing Yusuf Masarrah:) What do
                 you think, Yusuf Effendi?

Yusuf Masarrah: I don't blame al-Sulban, and I
                 don't try to understand his secrets and
                 mysteries, because I know that this is a
                 personal matter that affects him alone,
                 and I know that the morals of artists,
                 and musicians in particular, differ from
                 those of other people. And thus it would
                 be neither right nor fair for us to weigh
                 their actions on the same scales we
                 would use to understand the behavior
                 of others.

                 The artist—and by artist I mean that
                 talented one who creates new forms out
                 of his thoughts and feelings—is a
                 stranger among his family and friends,
                 a stranger in his homeland, even a
                 stranger to this world. The artist goes
                 east when people go west, and is
                 influenced by inner factors that he
                 himself can't explain. He is miserable
                 among the happy, happy among the
                 miserable, inept among the capable,
                 and capable among the inept. The artist
                 is above all laws, whether people accept
                 it or not.

Khalil Beik: What you are saying, Yusuf Effendi, is
                 no different in its message and tone

from what appeared in your article about the fine arts. And let me say again that this Western spirit, this foreign spirit that you preach, will be the reason for our destruction and extinction as a nation.

Yusuf Masarrah: Do you take what Bulus Effendi did last night to be an example of the Western spirit that you so reject and despise?

Khalil Beik: I am stunned by what Bulus Effendi did, and I say this with all due respect for his character.

Yusuf Masarrah: Doesn't al-Sulban have complete freedom to do with his voice and his art whatever he wishes whenever he likes?

Khalil Beik: Yes, he has every right to do whatever he wishes, but I also see that our social conventions do not support this kind of freedom. Our usual tendencies, our customs and traditions, do not allow one to do what Bulus Effendi did last night, not without putting himself in an awkward situation.

Miss Helanah: This is a delightful and meaningful debate. But since the reason for this debate is here among us, he can, of course, defend himself on his own.

Bulus al-Sulban (after a long silence): I wish that Salim hadn't started this conversation. I was actually hoping that what happened last night would disappear with last night. But if I'm in an awkward situation, as the esteemed Beik has said, then I can see why I should share my thoughts on the matter.

As you know, and I know this too, most of those who know me criticize me. Some say I'm spoiled, others say I'm a deviant, and there are some who say I'm unkind and that the unkind have no dignity. What is the reason, I ask, for this hurtful criticism? The reason is in my morals. Yes, my morals that I cannot change, and even if I could, I wouldn't. Why, I wonder, do people even care about me and my morals? Do they not have the choice to just forget about me?

There are, in this city, a lot of singers, chanters, musicians, a lot of poets and eulogists, incense bearers[29] and beggars, who sell their voices, thoughts, and emotions, even sell their own selves, for a dinar, a meal, or a bottle of liquor. The rich and the elite discovered this secret. That's why we see them buying the men of art and literature at the cheapest of prices and displaying them in their houses and mansions as they display their horses in the fields and their carriages on the roads.

Yes, gentlemen, singers and poets in the East are the incense bearers. No, they are the slaves, and it's been imposed on them to sing at weddings, chant at parties, mourn at funerals,

---

[29] Gibran refers to the Middle Eastern practice of carrying a censer and moving it in circles around another person's head in the belief that the smoke of the burning incense will protect that person from harm. These "incense bearers" usually utter sweet words or prayers for the person being perfumed, in hopes of money or some other reward.

and commiserate at cemeteries. They are machines that run in days of sorrow and nights of joy. Without a reason to mourn or to celebrate, they would be cast aside like goods without value.

I don't blame the notables and the wealthy. I blame the singers, poets, and authors who don't respect themselves enough to avoid being disgraced. I blame them because they don't rise above the vile and the low. I blame them for not preferring death to submission and humiliation.

Khalil Beik (inflamed): The people were begging you last night, and they tried in every way they could to get you to be kind enough to grant them a song or a chant. Do you take singing at Jalal Pasha's house to be a kind of submission and humiliation?

Bulus al-Sulban: If I could have sung at Jalal Pasha's house, I would have done it, but I looked around me and couldn't find among the guests anyone but the wealthy, who hear nothing but the ringing of dinars, and the notables, who don't understand anything of life except what lifts them up and brings others down. I looked around and couldn't find anyone who would know a Nahawand from a Rast, or an Oshak from an Isfahan.[30] That is why I couldn't open my heart before the blind or reveal the secrets of my heart before the deaf.

---

[30] These are all established styles of traditional Arabic music.

What is music but the language of the soul? Its unseen currents flow between the soul of the singer and the souls of the listeners. If there are no souls to listen and take in what they hear, the singer loses the impetus to speak and the motivation to disclose what his depths contain of turmoil and tranquility. Music is but a lyre with taut and sensitive strings. If these strings become loose, they lose their individuality and become like strands of linen. (He stands up and walks a few steps, and then says slowly:)

The strings of my soul were loosened in the house of Jalal Pasha when I observed the faces of the guests, men and women, and yet saw nothing but the false, the imposter, the imitator, the dull, the futile, and the arrogant. And their begging of me was nothing but the result of my silence and my reluctance. If I had been like so many of the other frog singers, no one would have even cared about me.

Khalil Beik (interrupting him, joking): And after that, you went to the house of Habib Sa'ada, and out of spite, just for spite, you kept singing until morning!

Bulus al-Sulban: I sat and sang until morning because I wanted to release the innards of my heart. I wanted to cast off a heavy burden from my shoulders. I wanted to rebuke the night, life, and time because I felt an essential need to re-tighten the strings that were loosened at the Pasha's house. And if you think, Khalil Beik, that I wanted to be spiteful, you are free to think as you like. Art is a free bird that swims and flies as he wishes and descends to earth when he wishes, and there is no force in this world that can chain him or change him. Art is a supreme spirit that can neither be bought nor sold. Easterners should know this absolute truth, and the artists among us—more rare than red sulfur—must honor themselves, because they are the goblets that God fills with heavenly wine.

Yusuf Masarrah: I agree with you, Bulus. And you have expressed my thoughts on this subject in a way that I myself cannot express. You are a son of the arts, while I am only one who researches it, and the difference between us is like the difference between sour grapes and aged wine.

Salim Mu'awad: Al-Sulban speaks the way he sings, and the listener has only to believe and surrender.

Khalil Beik: I am not convinced, and I will not be convinced. What is your philosophy but one of those dissipating illnesses from the Western countries.

Yusuf Masarrah: If you heard al-Sulban singing, Beik, you would be convinced and you would forget all about philosophy.

Maid (at this moment, the maid enters and addresses Miss Helanah): My lady, the kunafa[31] has arrived from the bakery, and I have set it on the table.

---

[31] Kunafa is a popular Middle Eastern dessert.

Yusuf Masarrah (stands, addressing all): Please, my brothers, we have prepared for you a tasty dish, very tasty indeed, almost Sulban-like in its flavor and sweetness!

(All stand, and Yusuf Masarrah, Khalil Beik, and Salim Mu'awad leave. Al-Sulban and Miss Helanah remain standing in the middle of the room, staring into each other's faces with an indescribable sparkle in their eyes.)

Miss Helanah (whispering): Did you know that I was listening to you last night?

Bulus al-Sulban (surprised): What do you mean, Helanah of my heart?

Miss Helanah (blushing and nervous): I was at my sister Miriam's house yesterday. I went to sleep at her house because her husband is away and she is afraid to be alone.

Bulus al-Sulban: Is your sister's house on the forest road?

Miss Helanah: And it's only one narrow lane away from Habib Sa'ada's house.

Bulus al-Sulban: And you heard me sing?

Miss Helanah: I heard the call of your soul from the middle of the night until dawn. I heard you until I heard God speaking.

Yusuf Masarrah (calling from a nearby room): Please, Bulus, the kunafa is getting cold.

(Bulus and Helanah leave.)

(Curtain falls)

5

IRAM OF THE PILLARS [1923] [32]

THE SCENE: A small grove of walnut, poplar, and
pomegranate trees surrounding a
solitary old house between the origins
of the river Assi and the town of al-
Hermel in northeast Lebanon

THE TIME: The afternoon of a July day in 1883

THE CAST: Zein al-Abidin al-Nahawandi,
a Persian dervish[33] in his forties,
known as The Sufi

Najib Rahmah,
a Lebanese man of letters, age 33

Amena al-Alawiyah,
known in the region as the jinni of
the valley.[34] No one knows her age.

---

[32] *Iram of the Pillars* appeared in Gibran's *Al-Bada'i' wa al-Tara'if*,
published in 1923 by Sadir, Beirut, and in Cairo by Yusuf al-Bustani.
Literally *Marvels and Anecdotes,* the title has also been translated as
The New and the Marvelous, Best Things and Masterpieces, and
Marvels and Curiosities. The play first appeared in English in a
translation by Anthony Ferris as *Iram, the City of Lofty Pillars* in *Secrets
of the Heart* (New York: The Philosophical Library, 1947), but not all
editions include the play. Another English translation appeared as *The
Many-columned City of Iram* in *Visions of the Prophet* (Berkeley,
California: Frog Ltd., 1997).

[33] A *dervish* is a Muslim ascetic.

[34] A *jinni* is a spirit capable of assuming animal or human form and
possessing supernatural powers. It is the origin of the English *genie.*

The curtain opens, and Zein al-Abidin appears, leaning on his arm in the shadow of the trees, drawing circles in the dust with his long walking stick. After a while, Najib Rahmah enters the grove riding a mare. He dismounts and ties the reins of the mare to a tree stump, and then shakes the dust off his clothes and approaches Zein al-Abidin.

Najib Rahmah: Peace be upon you, master.

Zein al-Abidin: Peace be upon you. (Then he turns his face away, saying to himself:) The greeting we accept, but as for the mastery, I am not sure whether to accept it or not.

Najib (looking around, asks): Does Amena al-Alawiyah live here?

Zein al-Abidin: This is one of her homes.

Najib: Do you mean, sir, that she has another home?

Zein al-Abidin: She has countless homes.

Najib: I have been searching since morning and have asked all those I meet about the residence of Amena al-Alawiyah, and no one has said that she has two houses or even more.

Zein al-Abidin: That's evidence that you haven't met anyone since morning but those who see only with their eyes and hear only with their ears.

Najib (confused): Perhaps the matter is just as you've said, but please tell me the truth, sir. Does Amena al-Alawiyah live here?

Zein al-Abidin: Yes, sometimes her body lives here.

Najib: Could you tell me where she is now?

Zein al-Abidin: She is everywhere (pointing towards the east), while her body wanders between these hills and valleys.

Najib: Will she be coming back here today?

Zein al-Abidin: She will be back if God so wishes.

Najib (sitting on a rock in front of Zein al-Abidin, studying him for a long time): It appears from your beard that you are a Persian.

Zein al-Abidin: Yes, I was born in Nahawand, raised in Shiraz, and educated in Nishapur. I have wandered the easts and the wests of the Earth, and I am a stranger everywhere.

Najib: We are all strangers everywhere.

Zein al-Abidin: No, by God, I have met and spoken with a thousand thousands of people, and I have seen only those who are confined to their surroundings and happy with their small pleasures, leaving the world to be in the narrow fragment they see of the world.

Najib (impressed by the words of his companion): The human being, sir, is created with an innate love for the place where he was born.

Zein al-Abidin: Limited people are inbred to appreciate what is limited of life, and the short-sighted cannot see more than a yard of the pathway he treads upon and a yard of the wall he leans his back on.

Najib: Not all of us have the ability to recognize the whole of life, and it is unfair to ask the short-sighted to see the distant and the tiny.

Zein al-Abidin: You are right, and you said it well. It is unjust to seek wine from unripe grapes.

Najib (after a moment of silence): Listen, sir, for many years I have heard tales of Amena al-Alawiyah, and these tales have affected me deeply. And so I decided to meet her, to ask her questions, and to know her secrets and mysteries.

Zein al-Abidin (interrupting): Is there anyone in this world who can know the secrets of Amena al-Alawiyah and her mysteries? Is there anyone among humans who can walk, strolling across the bottom of the sea as if in a garden?

Najib: I misspoke, sir. Forgive me. I cannot, of course, know everything about the mysteries of Amena al-Alawiyah, but I would like to hear from her the story of her entry into Iram of the Pillars.[35]

Zein al-Abidin: You would need only to stand at the gate of her dreams, and if it opened to you, then you will have reached your goal, and if it did not, then you are to blame.

Najib: What do you mean, sir, in saying that if it didn't open, I would be the one to blame?

Zein al-Abidin: I mean that Amena al-Alawiyah knows people better than they know themselves. She sees in a single glimpse what is in their minds, hearts, and souls, and if she found you worthy

---

[35] Iram is mentioned in the Quran (89:6-8): "Have you not considered how your Lord dealt with 'Aad—[with] Iram—who had lofty pillars, the likes of whom had never been created in the land?"

of speaking to, she would speak. Otherwise she would not.

Najib: What must I say and do to be worthy of hearing her speak?

Zein al-Abidin: It would be futile to try to approach Amena al-Alawiyah by word or deed. She does not and will not listen to what you say, nor look at what you do. She will hear with the ear of her ears what you do not say, and will see with the eye of her eyes what you do not do.

Najib (with signs of amazement showing in his face): How beautiful and eloquent is what you say!

Zein al-Abidin: What I say about Amena al-Alawiyah is nothing but the droning of a mute trying to sing a song.

Najib: Do you know, sir, where this remarkable woman was born?

Zein al-Abidin: In the bosom of God.

Najib (confused): I mean, where was her body born?

Zein al-Abidin: Near Damascus.

Najib: Can you tell me something about her parents and her upbringing?

Zein al-Abidin: How similar are these inquiries of yours to the inquiries of judges and lawmakers. Do you think you will comprehend the essence by asking about the accident,[36] or know the taste of the wine by looking only at the outside of the flask?

Najib: There is a bond between the soul and its body, and between the body and its

---

[36] "Accident," in this philosophical context, refers to the outer attributes of a subject.

75

surroundings, and as I do not believe in coincidences, I see that examining these bonds and their relationships is not devoid of benefit.

Zein al-Abidin: I like that. You have impressed me. It seems that you have quite a bit of knowledge. Then listen, I know nothing about Amena al-Alawiyah's mother, except that she died while giving birth to her daughter. As for her father, Sheikh Abdul Ghani the Blind, known as al-Alawi,[37] he was the most prominent of his age in mystical knowledge and Sufism, and he was—may God have mercy on his soul—extremely fond of his daughter. And so he educated and refined her, and poured into her soul the entire contents of his soul. And when she came of age, he found that the knowledge she had received from him was nothing like the knowledge that had been bestowed upon her, but rather like the foam to the sea. And so he said of her, "A light has emerged from my darkness to enlighten me."

And when she reached the age of twenty-five, he went with her on the Hajj.[38] When they passed through the Syrian desert and were three leagues from Medina, The Blind fell into a fever

---

[37] The last names are different because, in Arabic, a daughter of al-Alawi would be referred to as al-Alawiyah. In this context, both names indicate that they are descendants of Ali ibn Abi Talib, a cousin of the prophet Muhammad, and therefore of the most noble lineage among Muslims.

[38] The *Hajj* is a pilgrimage to Mecca.

and passed away, and his daughter buried him at the foot of a mountain.

She sat by his grave for seven nights, conversing with his soul, discovering the secrets of the unknown and asking to learn from it what lies behind the veil of life. On the seventh night, her father's soul inspired unto her that she should set her camel free, carry her food on her back, and depart from this place towards the southeast. And she obeyed. (He stops talking for a moment, gazes at the far horizon, then resumes:)

Amena al-Alawiyah kept moving across the desert until she reached the Empty Quarter Desert, which is the heart of the Arabian Peninsula that has never been penetrated by any caravan, and none have reached it but a few people, from the dawn of Islam to our present days. The pilgrims thought that she had gotten lost in this wilderness and fallen dead from hunger. Upon their return to Damascus, they told people of this, and she and her father were grieved by all who knew of their virtues. But later, their very mention slipped away from memory as if they had never existed.

Then, five years later, Amena al-Alawiyah appeared in Mosul, and her appearance, with all that she has of beauty, honor, knowledge, and righteousness, was similar to the falling of a star from space. She was walking unveiled among the people, standing beside the circles of scholars and imams, speaking of sacred matters, describing scenes of Iram of the Pillars with an eloquence never before heard by these people.

And when her tales became known and the number of her followers and pupils increased, the scholars of that city feared the beginnings of heresy and sedition, so they sent their complaints about her to the governor, who summoned her before him. He tossed a purse full of gold between her hands and asked her to leave the city. She refused the money but left the city by night without anyone accompanying her.

She went to Istanbul, to Aleppo, to Damascus, to Homs, and then to Tripoli. And in each of these cities, she stirred what had been at rest in the hearts of the people and ignited what had dimmed in their emotions. So they would gather around her and listen to her lectures and talks of her amazing experiences, attracted by powerful and magical forces. But the imams of religion and the scholars of knowledge in every country seized upon her words, refuted her teachings, and brought her before the rulers. After this, she sought isolation and came to this place years ago. She has lived in solitude, an ascetic in prayer, away from everything but the deepening of divine secrets.

This is just a little of all I know of the life of Amena al-Alawiyah. As for the knowledge that God has bestowed upon me about her spiritual being and about what lies within her of powers and talents, it is something that I cannot speak about now. Who among humans can collect in glasses and goblets the ether that surrounds this world?

Najib (deeply affected): Thank you, sir, for all you have so generously told me about this amazing woman. You have doubled my eagerness to stand before her.

Zein al-Abidin (looking at him for a moment): You are a Christian, aren't you?

Najib: Yes, I was born a Christian, and yet I know that if we stripped religions of the social and sectarian additions that have been attached to them, we would find that there is just one religion.

Zein al-Abidin: You are exactly right, and no human knows more about the absolute religious oneness than Amena al-Alawiyah. She is with all people, regardless of their different sects, like the morning dew that falls from on high and forms shining pearls among the petals of flowers that differ in color and shape. Yes, she is like the morning dew— (Zein al-Abidin suddenly stops talking and turns to the east, listening. Then he rises to his feet, pointing for Najib to take notice, which he does in obedience. Zein al-Abidin, whispering): There she is, Amena al-Alawiyah.

(Najib raises his hand to his forehead as though feeling a change in the particles of air. He then looks and sees al-Alawiyah approaching. His features change and his insides tremble, but he remains standing in place like a statue.)

(Amena al-Alawiyah enters and stands before the two men. In her stature, movements, and clothing, she more closely resembles the idol of an ancient people than an Eastern woman of the modern age. It would be difficult to determine her age by only observing her features, as the youthfulness in her eyes obscures a millennium of knowledge and experience. Najib and Zein al-Abidin remain rigid, awe-struck and reverent, as though they were in the presence of one of God's prophets. Al-Alawiyah stares into the face of Najib as though piercing his chest with her gaze. She approaches him, her features now relaxed and smiling, and speaks in a sweet voice.)

Amena al-Alawiyah: You have come to us, Lebanese, seeking our tales and to explore our circumstances, and yet you will not find in us but what you have in yourself, and you will not hear from us but what you have known in yourself.

Najib (emotional): Here I see, hear, believe, and am satisfied.

Al-Alawiyah: Do not be content with so little. He who approaches the fountain of life with an empty jar will return with two brim-full jars. (She extends to him her hand, which he takes with both hands in reverence and humble devotion, and he kisses the tips of her fingers, impelled by a hidden force. She turns to Zein al-Abidin and extends her hand to him, and he does as Najib did. She then steps back a bit and sits on a carved rock in front of her house. She points to a nearby rock and addresses Najib:)

These are our chairs. Sit. (Najib sits, and Zein al-Abidin does so as well.)

We see in your eyes a ray of divine light, and he who looks at us with the light of God in his eyes beholds our truth naked and undisguised, and we see in your face what devotion elevates from mere curiosity to a desire for the truth. If a word be upon your tongue, say it, and we shall listen. And if there be a question in your heart, ask, and we shall answer.

Najib: I have come to ask about a matter that people are talking about for how strange it is. But the moment I stood before you, I knew that life is but a reflection of the wholeness of the soul, and I am like a fisherman who cast his net into the sea to catch fish but in pulling it ashore finds within it a cache of precious stones.

Al-Alawiyah: You have come to ask us about our entry into Iram of the Pillars.

Najib: Yes, madam. Ever since my childhood, these three words, "Iram of Pillars," have haunted my dreams and tormented my imagination with what lies behind them of hidden symbols and implications.

Al-Alawiyah (lifts her head, closes her eyes, and with a voice that Najib feels is coming from the heart of space, she says): Yes, we reached the concealed city, and we entered it. We remained there and filled our souls with its fragrance, our hearts with its secrets, and our pockets with its pearls and jewels. He who would deny us of what we saw and know would deny himself before God.

Najib (carefully): And I, madam, am but a child who stammers in uttering what he seeks to explain. If I should ask you about something, I ask it in reverence, and if I should seek to understand a matter, I do so with care and devotion. Would you show your compassion for me, as an intercessor on my behalf, if I should exhaust your mystical being with too many questions?

Al-Alawiyah: Ask whatever you wish. God has made the truth with doors that open to all who knock with a hand of faith.

Najib: Did you enter Iram of the Pillars in body or soul? Is it a city made of the crystalized elements of Earth? Is it in a fixed and known place on Earth, or is it a spiritual city that reflects a spiritual state, one that the prophets of God might reach in a trance cast upon them by God like a veil?

Al-Alawiyah: What we see on Earth and what we do not see are but spiritual reflections. I entered the concealed city with my body, which is my visible soul, and I entered with my soul, which is my hidden body. And he who tries to separate the molecules of the body is surely astray. A flower and its fragrance are one thing. The blind who denies the color and form of a flower, saying, "A flower is nothing but a fragrance that hovers in the ether," is as the person

	with a cold who says, "What are flowers except forms and colors?"
Najib:	Then the concealed city that we call Iram of the Pillars is a spiritual state?
Al-Alawiyah:	Every space and time is a spiritual state. Everything that can be seen or comprehended is a spiritual state. If you would close your eyes and look into the depths of your depths, you would see the world in its wholeness and particles. You would experience its laws, know the reasoning that accompanies it, and you would understand the destinations of its journey. Yes, if you would close your eyes and open your inner vision, you would see the beginning of existence and its end, an end which in itself becomes a beginning and a beginning which transforms to an end.
Najib:	Can every human being close his eyes and see the pure essence of life?
Al-Alawiyah:	Every human being can desire and then desire and desire until that yearning removes from his sight the veil of what is external, and there he sees his own being. And he who sees his being sees the bare essence of life. Every being is the bare essence of life.
Najib (puts his hand on his chest):	Then everything in existence, that which can be sensed or comprehended, exists here, here within my chest?
Al-Alawiyah:	All that is in existence resides in you, with you, and for you.
Najib:	Can I tell myself that Iram of the Pillars exists within and not outside me?

Al-Alawiyah: Everything in existence resides in your core, and all of what is in your core resides in existence. There is no separation between the closest of things and the farthest, or between the highest and the lowest, or between the smallest and the largest. In a single drop of water are all the secrets of the seas. In a single atom are all the elements of Earth. In a single motion of thought are all of the motions and laws of the world.

Najib (with signs of confusion on his face): I have been told, madam, that you walked enormous distances before you reached that place known as the Empty Quarter in the heart of the Arabian Peninsula. And I was told that the soul of your father was your inspiration, guide, and companion until you reached Iram of the Pillars. In order to reach that concealed city, wouldn't the seeker have to be in a similar state to yours and have the physical and spiritual means to achieve what you achieved?

Al-Alawiyah: Yes, before we saw the walls of the city of God, we crossed deserts, suffered hunger and thirst, experienced the fear and heat of day and the terror and silence of night. But there were people who reached the city of God before us without walking a step and yet knew its beauty and magnificence without experiencing hunger in the body or thirst in the soul. Yes, by God, there were brothers and sisters of ours who traversed that sacred city without leaving the houses in which they were born. (She pauses a while, then points to the trees and fragrant plants surrounding them.)

Every single seed that autumn drops into the dust of the soil has its own special way of extracting the heart from the husk, and of creating from it its leaves, then flowers, and then fruits. Yet, however their ways may differ, the destination of all seeds will remain but one, and that destination is to stand before the face of the sun.

Zein al-Abidin (Swaying back and forth as though transported in spirit to a supreme realm, he then calls out in a gentle voice): Almighty Allah is the greatest! There is no God but Allah, the Generous, the Benefactor, who casts his own shadow between tongues and lips.

Al-Alawiyah: Yes, God is the greatest. There is no God but Allah. Say that there is nothing but Allah. (Zein al-Abidin mutters these words within himself while Najib, enchanted, stares at al-Alawiyah.)

Najib (in a voice almost a whisper): Nothing but Allah.

Al-Alawiyah: Say that there is no God but Allah and that there is nothing but Allah, and be a Christian.

Najib (bows his head, moving his lips, repeating her words, and then raises his head, saying): I said it, madam, and I will say it till the end of my life.

Al-Alawiyah: Your life has no end. You will survive along with the survival of all things.

Najib: Who am I and what am I that I should be immortal?

Al-Alawiyah: You are what you are. You are everything. For that, you will remain
immortal.

Najib: I am certain, madam, that the particles
that make up my ethereal body will
endure along with the survival of the
ethers, but I wonder whether that idea
that I call "I" will survive. Will that tiny
awareness that is shrouded in sleep
survive? Will these bubbles glistening
in the light of the sun remain, when the
waves of the sea that bore them are the
same waves that erase them to bring
forth new ones? Will these hopes and
dreams and joys and sorrows remain?
Will these illusions that tremble in
restless sleep remain in this strange
night with its great wonders, the
magnificent night with all its space,
height, and depth?

Al-Alawiyah (lifts her eyes to the heavens as though
retrieving something from the pockets
of space, and says in a firm tone full of
knowing, conviction, and mastery): All
that which exists survives, and the
presence of a being is the proof of its
survival. As for the idea[39]—which is
knowledge in its entirety, because
without it, even a man of wisdom would
not know if he exists or not—it is an
eternal, abiding, immortal being, which
does not change except to turn into
jewels, and does not vanish except to
appear in a more radiant image, and

---

[39] Al-Alawiyah is responding to Najib's question about "whether that
idea that I call 'I' will survive."

does not sleep except to dream of a more magnificent awareness.

And I wonder at the one who proves the survival of atoms in the outer layers that are perceived by the senses but denies that for which these layers are made. I wonder at the one who proposes the survival of the elements that create the eye and yet doubts the survival of the sight that takes the eye as its instrument. I wonder at the one who proves the immortality of the effects and yet insists that their causes disappear. I wonder at the one who is concerned with appearances rather than the reasons that form them. I wonder at the one who divides life into two halves and believes in the half driven forward while denying the driving force. I wonder at the one who looks at these mountains and plains that are flooded with the light of the sun, listens to the air as it speaks through the tongues of the branches, and drinks the fragrance of the flowers and herbs, and then says to himself, "No, it will not vanish, what I see and what I hear. No, it will not fade, what I know and what I feel. But this rational soul that sees and then fears and hopes, that hears and then becomes joyful and sorrowful, this soul that feels and then trembles and relaxes, that learns and then becomes saddened and seeks to explore—this soul that encompasses everything—will fade as the fading of the foam upon the face of the sea, and it will vanish as shadows before light." Yes, by God, I wonder at that being who is denying his own self.

Najib (excited): I believe in my being, madam, and he who hears you speak and does not believe is more a rock than a human.

Al-Alawiyah: God has placed in every soul a prophet to guide us to the light. But some people search for life outside of themselves while life resides inside, and yet they do not know.

Najib: Aren't there lights outside of ourselves without which we cannot reach what resides in our depths? Aren't there in our surroundings forces that awaken our strengths, and stimuli that alert the sleepers among us? (He lowers his head, hesitating for a moment, and then speaks again:) Didn't the soul of your father reveal to you things that are not known to those who are prisoners of the body and confined to the days and nights?

Al-Alawiyah: Yes, but it would be fruitless for the visitor to knock on the door of the house if there were no one inside to hear the knocks and open the door. What is a human but a being standing between the infinitude of his interior and the infinitude of his surroundings? Were it not for what we have inside, we would have nothing outside.

My father's soul conversed with me because my soul conversed with his and revealed to my mind what my subconscious knew. Without my hunger and thirst, I would not have had bread and water. Without my eagerness and

	yearning, I would not have found the object of my eagerness and yearning.
Najib:	Then could any one of us, madam, spin a thread out of his eagerness and yearning, and extend it between his own soul and the freed souls?[40] Is there not a group of people who have been granted the ability to converse with souls and apprehend their wills and aims?
Al-Alawiyah:	There are dialogues and nightly discussions between the inhabitants of the sky and the inhabitants of the Earth, continuing for as long as the cycle of days and nights goes on. There is no one who has not yielded to the will of these unseen, intelligent beings. How many are the things that an individual does, thinking he does them out of free will when in fact he is impelled. How many are the great ones of Earth whose greatness came from completely submitting to the will of a spirit among these spirits, like the submission of the lyre with sensitive strings to the playing of a skilled musician.
	Yes, between the realm of the visible and the realm of the mind, there is a pathway we cross in unconscious states that happen to us unknowingly. And then we return, carrying in our spiritual hands seeds that we cast into the soil of our daily lives, which grow into marvelous deeds or everlasting

---

[40] "Freed souls" meaning those who are no longer "prisoners of the body and confined to the days and nights" of the physical world (middle of previous page).

89

words. Without these open pathways between our souls and the ethereal spirits, no prophet would appear among people, no poet would stand among them, and no enlightened one would walk among them. (She raises her voice:)

I say, and the sources of the ages testify for me, that between the heavenly host and the people of Earth, there are bonds similar to the relationship of the commander to the commanded, and of the one who warns to the one who is warned. I say that we are surrounded with sentiments that attract our sentiments, and intelligent beings that counsel our minds, and powers that awaken our powers. I say that our doubts do not preclude our submission to that which we doubt, and our preoccupation with the desires of the body does not remove us from the influence of these spirits on our souls, and turning a blind eye to our true nature does not mask our true nature from the eyes of the veiled beings.

We, if we stand, are walking with their walking, and if we halt, we are yet moving with their movements, and if we be silent, we are speaking with their voices. Our sleep does not remove their awareness from us. Our waking does not remove their dreams from the stages of our imaginations. We and they reside within two realms housed within a single world, and two states joined within a single state, and two realities

	housed together in a single, whole, and eternal consciousness that has neither a beginning nor an end, neither an above nor a below, and neither limits nor directions.
Najib:	Will the day come, madam, when we will know through scientific research and cognitive experience what our souls know through imagination and what our hearts experience with yearning? Will the survival of the spiritual being after death be proven the way some of the secrets of nature have been revealed, and will we touch with the hand of abstract knowledge what we touch now with the fingers of faith?
Al-Alawiyah:	Yes, that day will come. But how far astray are those who realize an abstract truth with some of their senses and yet remain in doubt until it is shown to their other senses. How strange is he who hears the singing of the blackbird and sees it fluttering and moving, and yet remains in doubt about what he has heard and seen until he can take the body of the blackbird in his hand. How strange is he who dreams a beautiful truth and then tries without success to manifest it and embody it in the templates of the seen, and then doubts the dream, denies the truth, and holds suspect the beauty! How ignorant is he who imagines a thing and pictures it in its form and features, but when it becomes impossible for him to prove using shallow scales and verbal means, he believes the image to be illusion and the vision to be but emptiness.

Yet, were he to delve a bit deeper and contemplate for a moment, he would know that imagination is a truth that has not yet materialized, and that visualization is too superior a knowledge to be bound by the chains of scales, and too high and wide to be confined within the cages of terms.

Najib: Is there truth in every imagining, madam, and is there knowledge in every vision?

Al-Alawiyah: Yes, by God, the mirror of one's self does not reflect but that which stands before it, and should it wish otherwise, still it could not. The silent lake does not show in its depths the image of mountains, the painting of trees, or the shapes of clouds that do not exist in reality. And should the lake wish to do so, it could not. The elements of the soul do not reflect to you the echoes of sounds that the ethers do not reverberate with in reality. And if these elements wished to do so, they could not. Light does not cast upon the earth the shadow of any thing that has no being, and if the light should wish to do so, it could not.

What is faith in anything but the knowledge of it? And the believer sees with his spiritual sight what the investigators and excavators cannot see with the eyes of their heads, and he comprehends with his inner thought what they cannot comprehend with their learned thought. The believer experiences divine truths with senses that differ from the senses used by all people, and he thinks of those truths as a solid wall, and he goes on his way, saying, "This city has no gates."[41] (Al-Alawiyah stands and walks a few steps towards Najib, and in the tone of someone who has reached the end of his speech, and one who has no wish to add more, she says:)

The believer lives all of his days and nights, while the unbeliever does not live but a few seconds of it. How narrow the life of the one who lifts his hand between his face and the whole world and sees nothing but the lines of his palm. How great is my pity for the one who turns his back to the sun and sees only the shadow of his body upon the earth.

Najib (stands, sensing that the moment of his departure is approaching): When I return to the people, shall I say to them that Iram of the Pillars is a city of spiritual dreams, and that Amena al-Alawiyah walked to it along the path of fervor and entered it through the gates of faith?

Al-Alawiyah: Say that Iram of the Pillars is a true city that exists just as the mountains, woods, seas, and deserts exist. And say that Amena al-Alawiyah reached it after she crossed the Empty Desert and suffered the pain of hunger, the anguish of thirst, the sorrows of loneliness, and the horrors of solitude. And say that the titans of the ages

---

[41] Divine truth is as absolute as a solid wall but can only be perceived (entered) with the spiritual senses—it has no physical "gates."

erected Iram of the Pillars from that which was formed and crystallized from the elements of existence, and that they did not conceal it from the people but that people are the ones who have concealed themselves from it. He who fails to reach it, let him blame his guide and leader, rather than the difficulty or complexity of the road. Tell people that he who does not light his lantern sees nothing in the darkness but darkness. (She lifts her face high and closes her eyes, and a shroud of compassion and sweetness appears on her features.)

Najib (approaches her, bowing his head, and remains silent for a while. He then kisses her hand, whispering): Here the sun is setting, and I must return to the houses of people before darkness covers the road.

Al-Alawiyah: Walk in the light. Walk in the safety of God.

Najib: Madam, I will walk in the light of the torch that you have placed in my hand.

Al-Alawiyah: Walk in the light of the truth that cannot be extinguished by winds. (She gazes at him with a long and motherly look, then turns away from him and walks between the trees until she disappears before his eyes.)

Zein al-Abidin (approaching Najib): Where will you go now?

Najib: To the home of some friends near the origins of the river Assi.

Zein al-Abidin: Would you permit me to accompany you?

Najib: With pleasure, but I thought you would remain beside Amena al-Alawiyah, and my soul rejoiced with you and wished to be in your place.

Zein al-Abidin: We live by the light of the sun only from a distance, for who among us can live in the sun? (With a deeply meaningful tone:) I come once a week to be blessed and replenished, and when evening falls, I return content and satisfied.

Najib: I would love for all people to come once a week to be blessed and replenished and then return content and reassured.

(Najib unties the reins of his mare and walks with it alongside Zein al-Abidin.)

(Curtain falls)

6

THE MAN UNSEEN [1927] [42]

THE SCENE: A kingdom beyond the horizon

THE TIME: Beyond the clouds

THE CAST: The hunchback, the prime minister

Mubaraka, the prime minister's personal secretary

Bulus, another personal secretary

An attendant

A group of peasants

Prince Yusuf Khaldoon, representing capitalists

Two nuns

The unseen man

The scene: A room within the governmental suite of the palace. In the middle of the room, a large table sits with a great door behind it, a door to the right, and another door to the left. The room's furnishings are regal and majestic.

---

[42] Al-Qawwal notes that this play was from *Ad-Durar al-Mokhratra* [The Selected Pearls], a collection of essays by Gibran, Al-Rashidiyeh Press, Beirut, pages 58-80, and that it first appeared in the journal, *As-Sayeh,* in 1927. [Gibran also wrote this play in English, and Museo Soumaya has posted the unpublished (but incomplete) manuscript at http://gibrankgibran.org/eng/textos-ineditos/el-hombre-inadvertido]

It is evening.

The curtains open on the personal secretary, Mubaraka. With pen in hand and a stack of papers before her, she sits at the table awaiting the prime minister's arrival.

Bulus sits on the other side of the table.

Two guards stand, one at each side of the main door.

The prime minister enters from the door to the right, a hunchback with a deformed face, who seems more like a lion than a human. His extremities are two feet that he drags, and hands like two broken and shriveled branches.

The two attendants approach him and lift him onto a chair at the table. He lays his rough hands in front of him, trembling like dry reeds in the wind. Were it not for the echo in his voice, sounding as though it had come from the chest of a giant, one might think that he was a creature neither human nor ape, but one that had been mummified for some purpose, with a machine set inside him to activate his stiffened nerves. And yet there is a strange light in his eyes, a light that is not of the lights of this world.

Mubaraka and Bulus rise as he enters.

Mubaraka is a slender woman in her thirties, with ivory skin and auburn hair. Her clothes are white. The glimmer of wisdom shows in her eyes, and everything about her face suggests an exceptional personality, and everything about her character bespeaks order.

Bulus, a man in his forties, is dressed in a manner appropriate to the nature and mood of these meetings.

After lifting the prime minister onto his chair, the two attendants withdraw and stand at either side of the great door.

The Prime Minister (addressing Mubaraka): Sit, my child, sit. (He then turns to Bulus:) Come, please, sit.

    (After some silence:) Here we are again attending to work. No end to the work. No, the work never ends, not even in sleep. Who knows, we might even have to work after death. (He remains silent for a moment.) But tell me, Mubaraka, what have we to do today? I recall there are three or four problems we must address before the end of the day.

    (To Bulus:) Please note in brief all or most of what I dictate. You may need to review it tomorrow.

    (He turns back to Mubaraka:) Where shall we begin, my child, dear little friend of mine?

Mubaraka (looking at some papers in front of her): Sir, this is a letter from the Minister of Fine Arts.

The Prime Minister: Yes, yes, hand it to me.

    (Mubaraka hands him the letter, which he examines thoroughly. He then says:) What a lovely letter! In this minister's spirit, there is a lot of tenderness, in my opinion—a tenderness that exists between known and hidden laws. I did well when I assigned him to this position. (He looks again at the letter.) I wonder what I should say in response, how I should reply.

(He looks to Mubaraka:) Write this down:

Dear Sir:

Thank you for your gratifying and equally stimulating letter. All that you have so respectfully said about art in general, and beauty in particular, has touched me at a level beyond all levels. Yet will you permit me to say, and I'm neither a poet nor an artist, that beauty resides silently in the depths of every creature, even within the heart of life itself.

You and I cannot see beyond the veil of life, but were we able to reach beyond it, we would see only beauty. And we must not forget, my friend, that beauty resides within the enlightened ones, and in the forms designed by the hand of the greatest Creator—like a leaf that has fallen into your hand from a tree gilded by the gold of autumn, a rock that stands between you and the horizon, an infant playing and dancing in solitude, and an elderly one in the evening of day, gazing into the hearth's fire with a look that has never been of these days and nights.

I have no doubt that you will understand the meaning of my words, that beauty resides still and calm in the depths of our souls until it is awakened by our love. I have a desire to say more, but I fear to turn into a poet if I go too far, which would prevent me from being a servant of His Majesty the King, and that is not what I would wish to do.

Would you convey my greetings to your gracious wife and apologize on my behalf that I was unable to visit her garden? And will you tell her that the soul desires, but the body is unable?

Kindly, sir, accept deepest respect from

Yours sincerely,

(The prime minister sighs and turns to Mubaraka:) I have faith in this man. His artistic knowledge is not bound by the chains of the past. How hard it is for me to write to such a man without feeling the breath of youth quivering in my breast. How difficult it is to speak of art and beauty without becoming part poet. (After a moment of silence:) Hand me the other letter.

(Mubaraka hands him a letter which he takes and examines for a long time.) Yes, yes, this is from our politician friend, and a righteous man he is, although he doesn't know what to do with his virtue. How similar is he to a wealthy host waiting for his guests that never arrive. Let's reply to his letter. (He dictates to her:)

Dear Sir:

I have given a great deal of thought to the contents of your letter, and it revealed what in my own self I did not expect. Allow me to say this:

The might of the government is ascending, but on a single pillar—that which is the status of the lowest man in the government. Governments never have and never will rise above the people they govern, and the legislation you hope to enact is not legislation at all, but rather an inclination towards restriction and prohibition. And if you succeed in establishing that legislation, you will incite people to irritation and consequently to revolution. My heart was and will ever remain with the people who counter legislations with the white purity of their hearts. (Addressing Mubaraka:) Don't forget, Mubaraka, to write, "the white purity." (He returns to his dictation:) But such legislations are created by people who do not know purity.

Please convey my greetings to your dear mother. She was kind enough, two days ago, to send me a box of sweets. How precious these are because they were made by her hands, as she described in her lovely letter. I will write to her before the end of the day.

Kindly, sir, accept deepest respect from

Yours sincerely,

(He leans his head towards his chest and says:) I'm a little tired. I have grown weary, my child. And yet we have these papers before us, and we must work.

Mubaraka (in a voice filled with compassion and tenderness): This letter is from the archbishop, sir. Would you like me to read it to you?

(The prime minister takes the letter and looks at it. At this moment, a giant and majestic man appears from the right door, walking with firm steps and his head held high, towards the left door. He has a magnificent countenance and a shining face, like one who is not human but a soul of a finer and more sublime world. Among those in the room, no one sees him but Mubaraka. She stands up, frightened, and screams in a loud, deep voice. Papers and pens fall to her feet as she stretches her arms towards the giant and gazes at him with eyes full of wonder and awe. She then screams again like one who has had a vision. The giant disappears through the left door. Mubaraka falls back to her seat, but with the looks of love, faith, and reverence still in her eyes.)

The Prime Minister (drops the letter in his hands and asks Mubaraka): What happened, my child? What has come over you?

Mubaraka: Nothing. Nothing, sir. (She shuts her eyes and buries her face in her hands, as though trying to recreate the vision. A moment later, she takes a pen and paper and says to the prime minister): This letter, sir, how would you like to reply?

The Prime Minister (with an inquiring look): Are you tired from working? It has been a long day, but evening will descend shortly, and soon we will relax in the silence of the night. (In a voice of patience and endurance, he repeats his question:) Are you tired, my child?

Mubaraka: No, not at all. I have not become tired, and I won't be for as long as I work in your shadow.

The Prime Minister: Thank you. Thank you. Let's attend now to the letter of the archbishop. (And dictates to her):

Your Grace:

I inform you with deep regret that I will be unable to visit you and your diocese on Wednesday during the Good Friday holiday. As I see it, the truth is you would not want to place on your parishioners' shoulders the burden—I call it burden—of myself. You and they mistake me for a man who serves the government when, in reality, I am no more than a cart without horses.

I sense, kind sir, that you wrote not to me but to another man, a man who visits me from time to time, a man to whom I in my entirety am nothing but a hand—and I must say a paralyzed hand— despite the fact that I do believe that you wrote to me.

Forgive my absence, and permit me to visit you only in spirit next Wednesday to celebrate and pray with you and all of your parishioners.

May God sustain you.

Sincerely,

(Looking to Mubaraka:) I have become tired. I have grown weary, my friend. I am nothing now but a loose string in an old lyre. When this day ends, I will sleep a bit and another dawn will rise, and this lyre will be tuned by the greatest maker, and it will play melodies more lasting than the melodies of today.

(After a minute of silence:) I feel at this moment as though my heart is a tranquil lake and there is no breeze to write upon its surface what breezes wish to write on the surfaces or in the depths of lakes.

Mubaraka: Wouldn't you like to rest, sir, and leave the rest of the letters for tomorrow?

The Prime Minister: Tomorrow, tomorrow. Will tomorrow be any better than today, when today tries to run away from pain and hope? (At this moment, the attendant enters and bows before the prime minister, saying:)

Attendant: Sir, a delegation from the north is at the door, awaiting your permission to enter.

The Prime Minister: Yes, yes. These are righteous peasants. Tell them to come in.

(Three men enter, led by a dignified man. They stand before the prime minister and bow. Bulus takes a notepad to record what is said, while Mubaraka remains silent, watching with anticipation and interest.)

(The Prime Minister:) What can I do for you, my friends?

The Leader of the Delegation: Your Excellency, we represent the peasants of the north.

The Prime Minister: Yes, I know. What is your complaint?

The Leader of the Delegation: Sir, up until last year, the tax imposed on our fields was fair and acceptable, but this year they have raised the taxes on our livelihoods to an unbearable level. They have increased taxes on plowed and productive lands, and on those that are neither plowed nor productive. Our people are poor, and they feel now the burden of these taxes and see them as unfair. And they have put on our lips these words to present before you.

The Prime Minister: No, this is not fair. A government must not collect from you more than you earn. (He rubs his forehead with his hand, thinks for a moment, and then adds:)

I have an idea. Listen to me. Go back to your people and tell them, "The government burdens us by taxing every square foot of the land we own. We must cultivate every foot so that we don't deprive the government nor deprive ourselves."

Tell your people, "We and the government are in a race. The government has the authority, and we have the strength. Let's speed up towards the goal to see who wins. We run driven by our desire to work. Let the government run alongside us with all its troubles and ambitions. We greet the morning working, while the government rules.

We are not satisfied until we have poured our sweat into the fields, while the government finds its comforts entirely within its mansions— (He raises his shriveled hand and adds:) In mansions like this one.

Now go to your people and tell them to prepare for the race. If I am still here tomorrow, I will crown the winner with a laurel wreath upon his head. The winner will be he who leaves not an inch of land without plowing—he who waters it and cultivates it with his sweat. Farewell, companions.

(The delegation departs. After a quiet moment, the giant enters from the left door, walking in glory and dignity, and crosses the room with silent footsteps, gazing far away beyond the walls.)

Mubaraka (stands up, excited for the second time, stretches her arms towards him, and cries out, saying): O you who walks above the heads of men, o radiant one, stop a moment and look at me. Stop so that I can see your face. (The giant disappears behind the panels of the right door, and Mubaraka falls to her chair, muttering):

He disappeared! He disappeared again! He left! (The Prime Minister and Bulus look to Mubaraka intently and with concern.)

The Prime Minister: Tell me now, what has happened to you? What secret stirs within your heart? What did you see? Why do you let out all these cries?

Mubaraka (lifts her right hand from her eyes): Nothing happened, sir. Forgive me. Nothing happened at all. (At this moment, the attendant enters and, after bowing before the prime minister, says:)

Attendant: Prince Yusuf Khaldoon requests an audience, sir.

The Prime Minister: Let the prince enter. (He says to himself:) Now we must meet with silver-coated dust and converse with inherited honor. How I pity these noblemen who are on the brink of drowning but cling with all their might to the floating timbers, and yet they will sink to the depths. They will drown, and their heads will not rise above the foam of the sea.

Attendant (enters again, calling loudly): Prince Yusuf Khaldoon. (The prince enters.)

The Prime Minister (waves towards a chair beside the table, and the prince sits): Sir, you have come to tell me about the dispute between you and the peasants.

The Prince: Yes, and I have much to say in this matter.

The Prime Minister: I ask that you say nothing, but merely listen to what I am about to say to you. That is, if you might be generous enough to listen. Otherwise, please go to the field and hear the bees buzz as they carry nectar to the queen of the hive.

The Prince: Sir, I am all ears.

The Prime Minister (with great consideration and care): Princes and capitalists should take workers as partners. Before much

108

time has passed, each worker will become a partner with a share equal to the efforts he invests by his own hands. Princes and capitalists, therefore, lose nothing from the fruits of the land, whether oil or salt. A worker will feel contented and happy that he is a partner in all he reaps.

I have no more now to say, Your Highness. I hope that you understand my words and that after you leave you will act in accordance.

May God bless you with a fine evening, dear Prince. (The prince stands and bows before leaving.)

(To Mubaraka): I'm tired, my little one. My bow is still in my right hand, but nothing remains in my quiver except for a single arrow. The day nears its end. Come, tell me, what remains to be done?

Mubaraka: I remember, sir, that you promised to meet with the nuns, and they are waiting outside at this time. But if you prefer to rest, the nuns could meet with you tomorrow or the day after.

The Prime Minister: Sister Hannah, head of the convent. Let her come in.

Attendant (enters and says): Two nuns from The Savior convent are waiting in the hallway for your orders.

The Prime Minister: Tell them I am waiting for them. (The attendant leaves, and a moment later, a nun and her companion follow him into the room.)

(The prime minister, in a voice full of compassion:) Please come in and

109

have a seat. And forgive this body that cannot stand for you, but the soul stands respectfully before the servants of humanity. (The two nuns sit.)

Sister Hannah: How noble is my master, and how kind are such words.

The Prime Minister: Tell me, sister, what is it you desire? I hope that I can meet your need.

Sister Hannah: There is a property near our convent that we need for the orphanage, for those children without a known father or mother, for the children of chance, and the children of the night. But to our dismay, Prince Yusuf Khaldoon has laid his hand upon that land and occupied it without claim or justification. We wish for that land out of need, while the prince desires it merely to add to the vast properties he already owns. It is for this, sir, that we have come to you.

The Prime Minister (supporting his head with his hand): O mothers who never bore and yet sympathize with the children of mothers hidden behind the curtains of days, you have the right, and every right, to own a vast expanse in which to place a bed for a foundling. My heart was and still is with the women who search for the small, neglected heads, to pour upon them the nectar of the love in their hearts. I applaud you, sister, for you and your companions have found an object for love and tenderness. (He ponders in silence, then adds:) Let me think. Let me think for a moment.

There is a law in our country which states that, if more than fifteen years have passed over a field, vineyard, or grove, without it being farmed, planted, or inhabited, then the owner of that field, vineyard, or grove loses his right of ownership and it shall revert to the king. I will ask the King to grant you the land that you desire, in recognition of your humane service.

(Turning to Bulus:) Go to the library and search in a book called *Ownership and Claims*, and I think you will find in the seventh chapter how the king deals with abandoned land. Then write the argument and send it to My Lord the King, to affix his seal. (Bulus leaves the hall.)

Set yourself at ease, my sister. Be not concerned, o mother of motherless children. You have cheered me by allowing me to do you this favor.

Sister Hannah (rising with her companion): Thank you, sir. I thank you from the depths of my soul.

The Prime Minister: It is I who must thank you. Haven't you allowed me to be a father for a moment? (The two nuns trace the sign of the cross on their faces.)

Sister Hannah: May you be blessed and guarded by our mother Mary, Mary the Virgin, Mary, mother of all. May you be blessed by our Lord Jesus, Jesus our shepherd, Jesus who leads his flock to the green pastures. (The two nuns depart.)

The Prime Minister (lowers his head for a moment and says): What great women they are!

They plead for bread to feed the hunger of unknown hungry women. Yet we all stand begging at the door of the temple, and each of us begs to feed a different hunger.

(After a long silence, he motions for the two attendants to depart, then turns to Mubaraka, saying:) I've grown tired, child. I have become weary, my sweet friend. Here comes the darkness to cover us with its veil. (Mubaraka lights some candles in the hall, then comes back and stands beside her chair.)

The work of this day has ended, and you will rest from my debates until dawn, and after that there will be another day. Mubaraka, my friend, I am tired, and weariness has set its heavy hand upon my heart, but there are still many things I must do. There is a bridge to build, an edifice to erect, and in the depths of the night, there is a voice I must convey to sleepers. But I am tired. I am tired now. Good evening, Mubaraka, my little dear one.

(He lays his hands on the table, lowers his head, and heaves a long sigh. He then gazes into the face of Mubaraka and relaxes, and every movement of his body becomes still. At that moment, the glorious giant appears from the right door, walking this time to the middle of the room, where he stands upright like a column of light beside the silent corpse of the minister, laying his hand over him and gazing off into eternity.)

Mubaraka (looks at the giant, stretching her arms towards him, her face covered with magical rays. And with a voice that shakes the very corners of the palace, she says): I knew from the beginning that you were beautiful and dignified. I knew from the start that you are as you are revealed to me right now. O my friend, my beloved friend, how wonderful it would be if the whole world saw you as I see you now. How wonderful if all people knew what I knew and know right at this moment.

(Curtain falls)

7

THE KING AND THE SHEPHERD [1930] [43]

THE SCENE:	A green pasture amid the hills in the shadow of Lion Rock, in northern Lebanon
THE TIME:	Afternoon on one of the last days of summer
THE CAST:	The shepherd
	The king
	The king's minister

The shepherd sits in the shade of Lion Rock, watching his sheep with great satisfaction. He holds a nay[44] in

---

[43] Al-Qawwal notes that this play is from *Gibran Khalil Gibran,* by Mikhail Naima, Eighth Edition, Nofal Foundation, Beirut, 1978, pages 305-314.

Naima (in English, Naimy) begins this play with a note, saying that "This play was the last piece written by Gibran in Arabic. He had prepared it for a special edition of *As-Sayeh,* which was due to appear at the beginning of 1931, although it, too, had passed on just a few months before Gibran. That special edition was never released, and thus this story has not yet been published." Gibran died on April 10, 1931, and if *As-Sayeh* "passed on just a few months before," then Gibran probably wrote this play in late 1930 or very early in 1931. Naima's book first appeared in 1949, and its complete title (translated) is *The Complete Collection of Works of Gibran Khalil Gibran.*

[44] A *nay,* or *nai,* is an ancient reed flute, well-known in the Middle East and commonly associated with shepherds.

his hands and blows into it from time to time. A king arrives on horseback and looks at the shepherd.

The King: I notice you sitting comfortably in the shade of this rock. How strong is your weapon of contentment!

The Shepherd: How happy you must be on your horse's back, although I can see that you are tired.

The King (looking around him): Do you know who I am?

The Shepherd: No, but do you know who I am?

The King (laughing): If you knew who I was, you would faint in terror.

The Shepherd (holding a handful of dust): And if you knew who I was, you would die of happiness.

The King: How rude you are!

The Shepherd: How foolish and thick-headed you are!

The King: You should know who I am so you would take heed.

The Shepherd: And you should know who I am so that you would tremble in fear.

The King: I could kill you with the blade of my sword right at this moment if I wished.

The Shepherd: I could kill seven men like you with my staff if I wished.

The King (taken aback): Me? I am the king!

The Shepherd: And I, I am the shepherd of this flock.

The King: Are you mad?

The Shepherd: I didn't say I was the king of this land, so how can you call me mad?

The King: Do you not know that life and death
              rest between my lips?

The Shepherd: Then you are the one who killed my
              grandmother, and it was you who gave
              a child to a neighbor of mine, one of not
              yet fifteen years.

The King: No, I did not kill your grandmother, and
              I did not give a child to your neighbor.

The Shepherd: How then can you claim royalty? And
              how can you say that life and death
              rest between your lips?

The King: I wonder what you would do if you saw
              me surrounded by my soldiers?

The Shepherd: You see me now surrounded by my
              sheep, yet I do not see you doing any
              reasonable thing.

The King: What would you say if you saw me
              sitting upon my throne?

The Shepherd: Here I am leaning my back against
              this rock, and yet I've heard not one
              kind word from you!

The King (growing impatient): To Allah we belong,
              and to him we return![45] Man, do you
              not understand the meaning of the
              word, king?

The Shepherd: We are Allah! We are He to whom all
              aspire and return! Man, do you not
              comprehend the meaning of *shepherd*
              and *sheep*?

The King: Do you not understand our words,
              leader, chief, master, sultan?

The Shepherd (feigning impatience): Do you not
              understand our phrases, leader of the

---

[45] A common Arabic expression of vexation.

117

flock, head of the herd, master of the bull, guardian of the lambs?

The King: Do you not comprehend our words, land, kingdom, government, laws, crimes, punishments?

The Shepherd: Do you not comprehend the words, pastures, valleys, meadows, livestock, sheepfolds?

The King: It seems to me that you are not even a human.

The Shepherd: No, I am not a human if you are one of them. (At this moment, the king dismounts and approaches the shepherd menacingly.)

The King: I am the one who is king, and every king is like a father to each of his subjects. And as a father, I must teach you a lesson and thereby light your darkness. So I am now going to discipline you by force.

The Shepherd: How foolish you are! And how pompous are your claims! Even if you could teach me a lesson and light my darkness, you would not do it. Go now! Go! Be on your way! Go and find someone to discipline you and light your darkness. Then return to me, and if I find you qualified to be one of my subjects, I will direct you to the green pastures and sweet water springs.

The King (with forbearance): Be aware that this land is composed of kingdoms, and each has its own constitution.

The Shepherd (interrupting him): Yes, and kingdoms and constitutions are things that dangle from the mind, and your mind is feeble and divided into sects, some leading and some following—leading with arrogance and being led in humiliation.

The King: Be aware that people are either persons who rule or persons who are ruled. Leaders rule, and followers pay taxes.

The Shepherd: Dear God, is there anyone who would pay a tax to hear nonsense speak and watch ugliness flaunt and dance!

The King: People pay a price for superior minds to handle their affairs and lead them to the path of righteousness.

The Shepherd: Then you owe me half of what is on Earth, because, in spite of your stupidity and my impatience with you, I have led you to the right path.

The King: You must learn that each kingdom has laws. Some are divinely decreed, while others are agreed upon by the country's princes and chief scholars. He who follows them is protected, and he who rejects them will be punished and disgraced.

The Shepherd: It seems to me that your divine and earthly legislations are but a babbling nullified by the angels, but you're still unaware. If the people knew, they would hang you or imprison you until death rattles in you.

The King: You must learn, my ignorant son, that a philosopher and a shepherd stand as equals before these laws.

The Shepherd: And you must learn, my mummified grandfather, that a king and a beetle stand as equals before the face of the sun.

The King (forbearing): And you must learn that each kingdom has soldiers and officers that, when needed, invade and attack the enemies of the nation, and they will defend it when attacked by soldiers of a neighboring kingdom.

The Shepherd (laughs until he falls backwards): When the soldiers of my master the King and his aides invade a neighboring kingdom, whether justly or unjustly, I am the one who knows what my master the King and his aides do and where in relation to the army they can be found.

The King: I am telling you that the blade of the sword is made for enemies.

The Shepherd: Yes, the sword of the ignorant majority upon the neck of the lone individual. What cowardice! Did I not say once that the majority and cowardice are twins! Did I not say that once?[46]

The King (enraged): The ignorant majority? The lone individual? What are you saying? What you say will lead you to a place that will inspire you with words very different than these, and you will regret it. You will be remorseful and will weep bitter tears.

The Shepherd (laughing): Yes, I will have remorse for your babbling, and I will shed tears for your thick-headedness. I will feel remorse and will weep because the king

---

[46] Because "the majority and cowardice are twins" was not said earlier in the play, Gibran appears to be quoting a line that the reader is expected to recognize. The translators, however, have been unable to find any external reference.

of this land is a crippled rat. (At this moment, the king draws his sword, while the shepherd remains seated, holding his staff and saying with a laugh:) Hit me, you fool, for I shall not hit you first, and he who fights me is no better than a crowned rat.

The King (stands up): You are but a new joke, and meeting you has distracted us. We must go.

The Shepherd: And you are an old folly, and we are not pleased to meet you! Go now, and do not come back.

The King (smiling): Tell me, what else do you do here besides take care of these sheep?

The Shepherd: I see that you wish to talk. I do nothing but sit under the sun, and I watch my flock from time to time. But I do not deny, my idiot, that now and again every ewe raises its head to see whether I am here or not. That's all that I do here. But tell me, if you are one of the mighty talkers, who are you among the doers?

The King: Did I not say that I am the king of this land?

The Shepherd: You have nothing more royal in you than this odd-shaped rock. I have studied you, and I have found nothing but foolishness out of foolishness.

(Pointing towards the flock:) Do you see that ram, the one with the two big horns? I can tell you that he is not one of my better rams, and yet he has a strange habit of shaking his head every morning and looking up into space. Therefore, every time he walks, the other sheep and rams follow behind him. There are rams in my flock that are bigger than he is, in body and horns, but they do not lead the flock, for there is some honor in their nature. They avoid the honor of leadership, as if thinking that it is a form of lowliness.

The King: No one compares a king to a ram except an ignorant fool who does not know what he says and says what he does not know. We must forgive such an ignorant fool, for he does not know what he is saying. Words and actions are judged by intentions, and you know neither how to speak to princes nor to sultans, and a king and princes must understand this and have forbearance.

The Shepherd: I tell you, my little son, that when I compared you to the ram, I thought I was praising you more than you deserve. But what can we do with someone like you who cannot discern praise from ridicule!

The King (after looking carefully at the shepherd for a long time): You are no fool, man. No, you are not the fool that I'd thought. You belittle us with great intention, but I will not defile my hands with your blood. You should be killed, but by the sword of a man of your class.

The Shepherd (laughing aloud): By the hands of a man of my class? By the hands of a man of my same class? Oh foolish one, do you not know that, even if you search every corner of your false and stolen kingdom, you will never find a man of my class? I say "your false,

122

stolen kingdom." Do you understand me?

The King (scowling, with signs of fear on his face. He then acts as though angry and takes out his sword, screaming): Stand up and defend yourself, for I will now kill you for certain.

The Shepherd (takes his staff without moving from his place): My staff against your sword, brave man.

The King (strikes at the shepherd with his sword while the shepherd is still sitting): Take that, you vile wretch.

The Shepherd (stops the sword with his staff and, with a movement like magic, flings the sword from the hands of the king): Go and get your sword. Then come back to my staff again.

The King (goes, gets the sword, and walks slowly towards the shepherd): Did you not say that I stole my kingdom? Did you not say that? (He strikes at the shepherd again, but the shepherd blocks it again with the side of his staff, like a Persian cat playing with a mouse.) Why don't you stand up, you devil? You are most surely a devil, so why don't you stand up?

The Shepherd: Fight me while I sit, my little child, before you fight me while I stand. Isn't my sitting enough for you? (The king strikes at him for a third time, but the shepherd uses his staff to throw the king's sword a long distance.) Go and get your iron, Your Majesty.

The King (takes the sword and returns slowly with trepidation, as he can see that the shepherd is a wizard): I will kill you whether you are a human or demon.

The Shepherd (laughing): You can't kill a fly—you, a man stolen from the pockets of tomorrow. You are standing up, and I am sitting down, facing your sword with my staff. Come and hit me, you bravest of the brave. (As the king tries to hit him while the shepherd is laughing, the king hears a voice saying:)

Voice: Hey! Hey! (The king stops to listen.)

The Shepherd: There is someone calling your name. Praise be to God that my name is not Hey!

The King (answering): Hey! Hey!

The Shepherd: Oh listen, people. Kings and slaves call each other by the same name and in the same old, sick tone.

(They hear the sound of footsteps. The king returns his sword to his scabbard and stands by his horse, pretending to be calm, because His Majesty does not wish to be seen dueling with someone other than a king. At that moment, the king's minister arrives, armed to the teeth with every kind of hunting weapon.)

The Minister (halts a moment, quite surprised, and then gazes into the shepherd's face. Once he is sure, he falls to his knees, saying): My Prince! Oh my Prince, you are alive!

The Shepherd (looks at the minister and smiles): Here is my old friend who acted like a strong horse at my grandfather's house and had me riding on his back while he jumped, neighed, and played. Look at him now, carrying the weapons of the king of the land! And why not? Everyone improves and advances. That is, if he gives thought to it. But I doubt the improvement of that one who calls himself king.

The Minister (to the shepherd): Oh my lord, it is wonderful to see you again.

The Shepherd: Do not utter such words so loudly. His Majesty might hear you.

The King (to the minister): Who is this impudent man that makes you fall to your knees before him and address him as Prince? Who is this arrogant wretch?

The Minister: He is my master, Dhaher al-Saadi, one of the three Saadian princes, the remaining leaves on the branch of that ancient tree.[47] Pray listen, my King. Consider how he now cares for a flock of sheep, while his brother is in the Assi valley plowing the land, and the third brother built a textile mill at the foot of this mountain to weave cotton and flax.

The Shepherd (shaking his head): And so it is we who are still kings. Now leave me alone, and forgive me.

(Curtain falls)

---

[47] It is unclear whether the Saadian princes are fictitious or historical. One possibility is the lineage of Sa'd, the brother of Dhaher al-Omar, the ruler of northern Palestine in the 1700's. Given Gibran's quotation, "the majority and cowardice are twins" (page 120), some historical reference seems likely.

ILLUSTRATIONS

The border of the front cover of this book is based on a floral design that Gibran developed at the age of only 14.[48] The design also appears at the bottom of the back cover. It was multiplied and embossed for a collection of over a dozen titles by the well-known Belgian author, Maurice Maeterlinck. Originally written in French, the series was published in English by Dodd, Mead and Company of New York. An example is the volume pictured opposite, which was printed in 1902, and Gibran considered the work to be "a masterpiece."[49] It is green with gold lettering, 5 ¼ x 7 ¾ inches.

---

[48] Jean Gibran and [cousin] Kahlil Gibran, *Kahlil Gibran, His Life and World* (New York: Interlink Books, 1998), 64.
[49] *Ibid.*, 57.

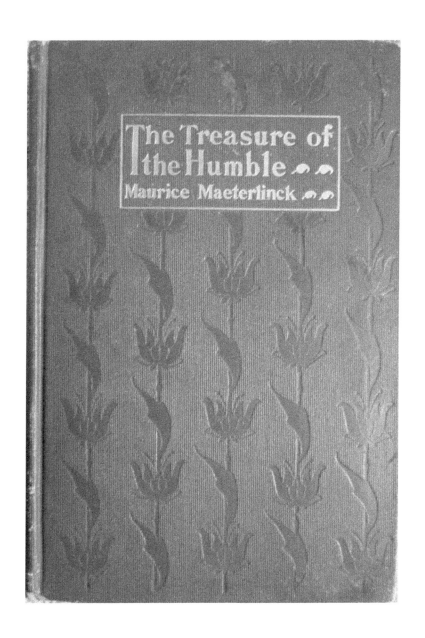

The Treasure of
the Humble
Maurice Maeterlinck

The walking figure on the front cover of this book is a detail from an original design by Gibran, whose signature appears in Arabic below the right heel. It served as the cover illustration for the January 1921 edition of *As-Sayeh* (The Tourist).[50] Most of Gibran's Arabic plays first appeared in that journal, which was published in New York from 1912-31. Opposite is a photograph of the entire design, presented courtesy of the Peter A. Juley & Son Collection, Smithsonian American Art Museum, Washington, D.C.

---

[50] *Ibid.,* 344.

The upper back cover of this book is based on a design by Gibran that adorns a small volume of poetry by Lilla Cabot Perry, published in 1898 by Copeland and Day (opposite).[51] Besides being a publisher, Fred Holland Day was a prominent Boston photographer and a key figure in Gibran's early life.[52] Measuring 4 ½ x 7 inches, the cover is in two shades of green, with gold flowers and lettering.

---

[51] That Gibran designed it is established by the cousins, Jean and Kahlil Gibran. *Ibid.*, 65.
[52] *Ibid.*, 37-68.

CPSIA information can be obtained
at www.ICGtesting.com
Printed in the USA
LVHW031217301018
595340LV00001B/92/P